Goddess Flourishing

Celebrating the Sacred Feminine in Modern Life

Emeleth Morliniel

Woolmonger Publishing

Dedication

This one is for the readers, for all those women who want to step out of their comfort zone despite feelings of insecurity – and dance. Find your inner muse, and become her. Hail Terpsichore!

Table of Contents

Preface

Fat Girls Don't Dance

I went from looking six to looking sixteen over the summer between the fifth and sixth grades. Puberty didn't so much arrive as it smote me. There was no training bra phase, I went straight into a size 36C and was summarily chastised about how it was my job to keep my body from being too sexualized in the male gaze. With those newfound curves came ever increasing body weight. And as was the way of life in the 1980s, I was fat shamed.

We all know this story. Try as I might, no matter how little I ate or how active I was, I couldn't stop the weight gain. I internalized the stigma. I was The Fat Girl.

There was a time during the early 90s when my family lived in Berea, Kentucky. Berea College used to host street dances for country dancing, and so one evening I walked to the center of town and joined in the festivities. I was in love with it! Dancing is the only physical activity that has ever kicked in the endorphins for me. I was high on my own neurotransmitters. I lost my self-consciousness and simply let my body enjoy the thrill of the movement. I went to more than one country street dance that summer, and I couldn't get enough.

At some point, someone must have seen me dancing and been somehow offended that I was flaunting my corpulent flesh in public. Perhaps by jiggling? I was modestly clothed for a summer night in Kentucky, in a long skirt and short sleeve shirt that covered my cleavage. People back then were always offended by a busty woman's cleavage.

I honestly don't know what conversations went on out of my presence, and it doesn't really matter. What matters is that I was told, by someone who should have had my best interests at heart, that "Fat girls don't dance."

What in the age of Jazzercise and obsessive aerobics fitness classes led anyone to that conclusion seems illogical now, in 2024. Now we think of dance as a great workout. But back then we didn't have the body positivity movement that we have now. Tough love was still seen as the way to get people to change to suit society. And some of my loved ones said some really tough things to me about the size and shape of my body.

I did what most young women in their late teens might do, I took those words to heart. I made it part of who I was, part of my internal social policies, part of the way I went about being in the world. I stopped dancing, not just in public but in front of any other humans. (Although cats have never seemed put out by the sight of a curvy girl shaking what the goddess gave her, merely bemused at silly human behavior overall.)

Fat girls don't dance became so enmeshed with my identity as The Fat Girl that it affected the way I moved my body entirely. I tried not to take up so much space, not to let my chest bounce when I walked, not to inflict the sight of my fatness on the world. None of that was healthy, of course. And I didn't dance for nearly 30 years.

There is one exception. There was a man who asked me to dance for him, and he showered me with such adoration that I acquiesced. It was special, I was in love, and the vulnerability felt like hot lava coating my skin. He told me recently that he felt extremely honored and it remains one of his favorite memories of us back then. Funny how people can remember an event differently. The thought that I was too plump never entered his mind.

Fast forward to the summer of 2018 when I joined the cast at the renaissance faire. This was after decades of growth, and having finally left and gotten over a psychologically abusive relationship with someone who made me feel like I was in a state of constant rejection for not being good enough. Following much cajoling from friends and a great many tears, I became part of the cast dance troupe.

It was like finding a lost love. I was learning folk dances and having the time of my life. And as part of a group in which the majority of the women were also quite curvy, I was less concerned with how I looked to others and allowed myself to delight in the moment. The group's philosophy was that anyone could dance with us – in fact it was encouraged – whether they were a good dancer or not, as long as they were having fun. We regularly recruited patrons to the faire to dance with us. And in the character I created I was able to let the role be my mask and shed the trauma of fat girls don't dance. Runa is bold. Runa asks the popular guys to dance. Runa was in a photo that was featured in a nation-wide magazine, dancing with the most popular guy that season. And it was not flattering. I weighed about 300 pounds at the time. I didn't care, and still don't.

The next year, I took over as director of the renfaire dance troupe, the previous director having retired from a decade as part of the cast. And the year after that my dancers pulled off a flying rose! It's a group lift in the more difficult version of the Levi Jackson Rose that I had first seen performed by the Berea College Country Dancers. The dancers circle up and the ladies pick their feet up and are carried along by the men as the whole circle spins. For perspective, I've seen Riverdance and Celtic Woman perform this move. It ain't easy. And yet I was able to teach it to my little group of nerds and misfits through the power of positive vibes and friendly encouragement. I was the dance director at that faire for five years, and then happily handed over the job to my very capable assistants.

Fat girls don't dance? Hell yes they do! And they have a great time doing it.

In the interest of full disclosure, and in case anyone reading this sees me these years later, I have lost a lot of weight since I first let myself dance again. With a lot of hard work, tracking everything I ate on Weight Watchers, medical supervision, and pharmacological intervention, I have shed about 200 pounds. Don't at me for humble-bragging. I'm diabetic and this healthy change probably extended my life by about 15 years. And no shame on the curvy women out there, you are beautiful too.

Despite the tag in my jeans saying size 4, in my mind I'm still The Fat Girl. I am always one emotional crash away from binge eating an entire pizza. And I notice how others, especially strangers, treat me differently now. I suddenly acquired pretty privilege at the age of 53, and as a sociologist I can tell you that I understand all the subtle nuances of what that means. Sometimes the cognitive dissonance is striking.

I love to dance! Dancing has become part of my self-concept and my social identity. It's part of who I am now. Don't ever let anyone else tell you that you can't do something because it offends their sensibilities. Embrace your inner goddess and let her propel you forward until you embody every bit of your personal power. And, as the song says, I hope you dance.

Dress well and fight for the light!
Em, 2024, somewhere in the wilds of central Kentucky

Unveiling The Sacred Feminine

Defining the Sacred Feminine

Exploring the Sacred Feminine invites us to engage deeply and thoughtfully with the profound and multifaceted nature of femininity as a spiritual and cultural concept that transcends both time and geography. This concept resonates across various traditions, belief systems, and cultural narratives, weaving a rich tapestry of meaning. At its core, the Sacred Feminine embodies essential qualities such as intuition, nurturing, creativity, and wisdom—qualities that resonate deeply within each of us. These attributes foster a sense of connection to our own inner selves and enhance our understanding of our unique identities in a world that often seeks to define us narrowly.

The principles of the sacred feminine are often rooted in various spiritual, philosophical, and cultural traditions. While interpretations may vary, several core principles are commonly associated with the sacred feminine. The foremost of which is nurturing. This principle emphasizes the importance of caring, compassion, and support. The sacred feminine embodies qualities of nurturing that promote healing and growth, both in individuals and within communities. With this comes emotional expression, emphasizing the importance of emotional authenticity, this principle encourages individuals to express their feelings openly and honestly. The sacred feminine values vulnerability and the strength that comes from embracing one's emotional landscape.

Another innately feminine characteristic is intuition. The sacred feminine encourages the development of intuition and inner wisdom. This principle suggests that individuals are encouraged to trust their instincts and feelings as valid sources of knowledge, often valuing emotional intelligence alongside rational thought. Closely tied to that is spirituality and sacredness. The sacred feminine encourages a deep spiritual connection that transcends traditional religious boundaries. This principle invites individuals to explore their own spirituality, often emphasizing the divine within themselves and the sacredness of all life.

We could hardly discuss femininity without mentioning creativity and fertility. This principle celebrates creation in all forms—art, life, ideas, and relationships. The sacred feminine is often associated with fertility and the generative forces of nature, reflecting the ability to bring forth new life and innovation. So too is a connection to nature. The sacred feminine recognizes the interconnectedness of all life and the importance of living in harmony with the natural world. This principle promotes sustainability and respect for the earth, highlighting the cyclical rhythms of life.

In today's world, women are seen as more social than men. Women build communities, women connect. We see this in sacred femininity as well. The sacred feminine highlights the importance of relationships and communal bonds. This principle fosters cooperation, support, and collective action, encouraging a sense of belonging and shared purpose. Born of these connections to community comes wisdom and eldership. This principle honors the wisdom that comes with age and experience. The sacred feminine recognizes the value of listening to the voices of women and elders, acknowledging their insights and contributions to society.

Empowerment is often misunderstood. This does not mean always having to take charge, to lean into status, or to be in control of every situation. The sacred feminine advocates for justice, equality, and the recognition of the inherent worth and capabilities of all individuals. Empowerment is tempered by balance and harmony. This principle advocates for balance between the masculine and feminine energies within all individuals and societies. It emphasizes the need for equilibrium in various aspects of life, including work and play, logic and intuition, and independence and interdependence reverence and mirth.

These principles collectively represent a holistic approach to understanding the sacred feminine, promoting a worldview that values connection, creativity, and compassion. They serve as a guide for personal growth, community building, and spiritual exploration.

These essential qualities are often illustrated through a diverse array of goddess archetypes that have emerged throughout history, with each serving as a powerful symbol of strength, resilience, and empowerment. These archetypes reflect the intricate and diverse aspects of womanhood, inspiring women from all walks of life to reconnect with their intrinsic power and divine essence. This reconnection not only fosters a sense of identity but also encourages profound personal growth and self-empowerment, enabling individuals to navigate the complexities of their lives with confidence.

By delving into the vast array of goddess figures across different cultures—such as the nurturing Earth Mother, the fierce and courageous Warrior Goddess, the wise and insightful Crone, and the transformative Maiden—we can gain a more nuanced understanding of the complex and dynamic nature of the Sacred Feminine. This exploration highlights its profound significance in our contemporary lives and offers insights into how these archetypes can guide and inspire us. This journey enriches our spiritual paths, deepens our connections to one another, and shapes our personal identities in meaningful and transformative ways. Engaging with the Sacred Feminine invites us to honor these diverse aspects of femininity, fostering a collective consciousness that celebrates the empowerment and agency of all individuals.

Practices of feminine spirituality play an essential and transformative role in honoring the Sacred Feminine while simultaneously deepening our connection to our inner selves and to each other. By engaging in a rich tapestry of rituals, meditations, and sacred ceremonies, women are empowered with invaluable tools that enable them to access their intuition and unleash their creativity, thereby facilitating profound personal reflection and transformative growth. These spiritual practices can encompass a wide range of activities, from simple yet powerful daily affirmations that uplift the spirit and reinforce positive self-belief to more elaborate and meaningful ceremonies that celebrate the cycles of the moon, the changing seasons, or significant life transitions, such as pregnancy or important rites of passage.

As women actively participate in these rituals, they not only cultivate a deeper sense of community and sisterhood but also establish sacred spaces that encourage the sharing of experiences, collective healing, and mutual empowerment in a supportive environment. Thus, feminine spirituality honors not just the individual journey of each woman, enriching her personal growth, but also the shared experience of womanhood, fostering a collective sense of identity, purpose, and interconnectedness.

This deep connection greatly enriches our lives, allowing us to thrive together in harmony, celebrating our diverse paths while standing united in our shared experiences. The act of coming together in these spiritual practices strengthens our bonds, creating a powerful network of support and inspiration. Each ritual and ceremony becomes a catalyst for deeper understanding, compassion, and the celebration of our unique expressions of femininity. In this way, feminine spirituality not only nurtures the soul but also empowers women to embrace their authentic selves while weaving a vibrant community tapestry that uplifts and inspires all.

The themes of healing and empowerment through the Sacred Feminine serve as the cornerstone of this profound exploration, inviting women to delve deeply into their own journeys. As they navigate the diverse and often tumultuous phases of life, women frequently encounter challenges that can feel isolating, daunting, and overwhelming, creating barriers to their personal growth. Embracing the Sacred Feminine not only fosters a sense of community among women but also allows them to find solace and strength in the ancestral wisdom and powerful archetypes that resonate with their unique and individual experiences. Techniques such as journaling, visualization, meditation, and energy work can significantly enhance the healing process, empowering women to reclaim their narratives, rediscover their identities, and build remarkable resilience.

This transformative journey often requires confronting deeply ingrained societal conditioning and cultural narratives that have historically marginalized the female experience, opening pathways for true self-discovery. By courageously doing so, women can uncover the immense strength within themselves to rise, affirming their rightful place as powerful, nurturing beings in a world that often seeks to diminish their invaluable contributions and silence their voices. Through this reclamation and shared experience, women can inspire one another, generating a ripple effect of empowerment and healing that extends far beyond their individual lives and into their communities, fostering collective strength and unity.

Studying mythology offers invaluable insights into the intricate principles of the Sacred Feminine, revealing how these rich and diverse narratives have profoundly shaped our understanding of femininity throughout history. Myths and legends from a wide array of cultures encapsulate the myriad challenges and triumphs experienced by women, reflecting the societal values and spiritual beliefs that have evolved across generations. By thoroughly examining these complex and multifaceted stories, we can extract timeless lessons about love, sacrifice, strength, resilience, and the cyclical nature of existence itself.

Engaging deeply with these powerful narratives not only enhances our appreciation of the Sacred Feminine but also enables us to draw meaningful connections between ancient wisdom and contemporary experiences, enriching our understanding of both. This profound engagement fosters a deep sense of continuity that resonates through the ages, inviting us to reflect on our own lives in relation to these enduring themes. The exploration of mythology not only broadens our perspective on femininity but also encourages us to embrace the wisdom of our ancestors as we navigate the complexities of modern life.

Today, the Sacred Feminine manifests vibrantly and powerfully in the lives of women who embody its essential principles through a multitude of avenues, including activism, creativity, and self-care practices. As women reclaim their inherent power and amplify their voices, they courageously redefine traditional notions of success, health, and beauty on their own terms, boldly challenging the societal norms and expectations that have long dictated their roles within society. The ongoing dialogue surrounding women's health, body image, and fertility increasingly incorporates a profound acknowledgment of the Sacred Feminine, promoting a holistic approach that honors not just the physical body but also the spirit that resides within each individual. By embracing this empowering perspective, women can cultivate a deeper appreciation for their bodies and their unique life paths, enabling them to uplift themselves and their communities in meaningful and transformative ways.

In joyful celebration of the Sacred Feminine, we honor and respect our individual journeys while weaving a rich, shared narrative of strength, resilience, and divine femininity that echoes through the ages. This celebration not only enriches the tapestry of human experience but also illuminates the path for future generations. It ensures that the values and lessons of the Sacred Feminine continue to inspire and empower those who follow, creating a lasting legacy of empowerment and transformation that resonates across time and space. By recognizing the significance of these values, we contribute to a more inclusive and compassionate world, where every woman feels valued and empowered to express her true self, fostering a collective spirit of unity and strength that echoes throughout history

Historical Context and Evolution

The sacred feminine has long served as an essential and vital aspect of human spirituality and cultural expression throughout the entirety of history, often acting as a mirror reflecting the diverse roles, profound reverence, and immense power that women have held in various societies around the world. From the ancient matriarchal cultures that celebrated goddess figures as potent symbols of fertility, wisdom, and creation, to the patriarchal systems that sought to suppress, diminish, and obscure these vital representations, the evolution of the sacred feminine unfolds as both intricate and dynamic. By closely examining the rich historical context surrounding goddess archetypes, we gain a deeper understanding of how these powerful figures have not only shaped but have also been shaped by the societies that revered and celebrated them. This exploration offers valuable insights into our own spiritual journeys today and encourages a reawakening of the sacred feminine within contemporary contexts, highlighting its relevance in modern life. As we delve deeper into the narratives and symbols that have been woven throughout time, we uncover layers of meaning that reveal the enduring significance of the sacred feminine and its ongoing relevance in our lives.

This journey invites us to reconnect with the myriad aspects of femininity that have been celebrated and, at times, marginalized or overlooked, allowing us to appreciate the complexity and richness of women's roles throughout history. By recognizing the profound impact of these archetypes on our collective consciousness and spiritual well-being, we open ourselves to a renewed understanding of femininity that transcends cultural boundaries and resonates powerfully with our current spiritual quests, illuminating pathways toward healing, empowerment, and a deeper connection to the divine feminine. As we embrace this deeper understanding, we empower ourselves to acknowledge and honor the legacy of the sacred feminine, fostering a more inclusive spiritual landscape that values the contributions and wisdom of women from all walks of life.

In early civilizations, such as those in Mesopotamia and ancient Egypt, goddesses played a central and vital role in shaping the understanding of fundamental concepts like life, death, and rebirth. Figures such as Inanna and Isis not only embodied the divine feminine but also represented a complex and intricate interplay of qualities, encompassing both the nurturing aspects of motherhood and the fierce, indomitable power associated with transformation and protection.

The Greek and Roman goddesses portray the divine feminine through a rich tapestry of mythology, symbolism, and cultural significance. These deities reflect various aspects of femininity, including love, wisdom, war, fertility, and the natural world, each contributing to a multifaceted understanding of womanhood.

In Greek mythology, Aphrodite stands as the goddess of love and beauty. She represents desire, passion, and the complexities of romantic relationships. Her origins, often depicted as emerging from the sea foam, symbolize the unpredictable and transformative power of love. Aphrodite's influence extends beyond mere attraction; she embodies the idea of love as a force that can inspire creativity and connection.

Athena, another prominent figure, represents wisdom, strategy, and warfare. Unlike many other goddesses, she is known for her intellect and rationality, showcasing the strength of the feminine spirit in realms traditionally dominated by men. As a virgin goddess, Athena embodies independence and empowerment, serving as a protector of heroes and cities, which highlights the nurturing yet formidable aspects of femininity.

Demeter, the goddess of agriculture and fertility, embodies the nurturing aspect of the divine feminine. She symbolizes the cycles of nature, motherhood, and the sustenance of life. Her relationship with her daughter Persephone reflects themes of love, loss, and the resilience of women. This myth illustrates the deep connection between women and the earth, emphasizing the vital role of femininity in sustaining life.

In Roman mythology, Venus takes on the mantle of love and beauty, paralleling Aphrodite. She showcases the sensual and nurturing aspects of femininity, but also possesses a fierce protective quality, particularly in her role as a mother. Venus's influence extends into the realms of art and culture, where she inspires creativity and passion.

Minerva, the Roman counterpart to Athena, embodies wisdom and strategic warfare. She is often depicted as a warrior goddess, representing the strength and intellect of women. Minerva's association with crafts and the arts further underscores the idea that femininity encompasses both strength and creativity, highlighting the diverse capabilities of women.

Goddesses like Artemis and Diana represent independence and the untamed spirit of womanhood. As goddesses of the hunt and wilderness, they embody a connection to nature and the freedom found in solitude and self-reliance. Their fierce protection of the vulnerable showcases the nurturing side of the divine feminine, reinforcing the idea that women can be both protectors and warriors.

Greek and Roman goddesses collectively reflect the complexity of womanhood, encompassing love, wisdom, strength, and nurturing. Through these deities, ancient cultures celebrated the multifaceted nature of femininity, offering timeless archetypes that continue to resonate in contemporary discussions about gender and identity.

Celtic and Norse goddesses embody the divine feminine through their diverse roles, attributes, and influences in mythology and culture. Both traditions, while distinct, share common themes in their reverence for nature, fertility, war, and wisdom, illustrating the multifaceted nature of femininity.

In Celtic mythology, goddesses such as Brigid, Danu, and Morrigan exemplify various aspects of the divine feminine. Brigid, often associated with fire, poetry, and healing, represents the nurturing and creative forces of the feminine. She is celebrated during Imbolc, heralding the arrival of spring and symbolizing rebirth. Danu, considered the mother of the Tuatha Dé Danann, embodies the earth and fertility, often interpreted as the source of life. The Morrigan, a more complex figure, embodies war and sovereignty, suggesting that the feminine can also be fierce and powerful. She often appears as a triple goddess, showcasing the multiplicity of womanhood, encompassing maiden, mother, and crone.

In Norse mythology, goddesses like Freyja, Frigg, and Hel illustrate similar complexities. Freyja, a goddess of love, beauty, and war, commands a duality of nurturing and fierce independence. She is a warrior who rides into battle and a symbol of fertility, showcasing the strength inherent in femininity. Frigg, the wife of Odin, embodies wisdom and motherhood, highlighting the protective and guiding aspects of the feminine. Hel, ruler of the underworld, represents the acceptance of death and the cyclical nature of life, emphasizing the transformative power of femininity.

Both Celtic and Norse goddesses serve as guardians of the earth and its cycles, reflecting the deep connection between women and nature. They represent the nurturing and life-giving aspects of the feminine while also acknowledging the strength and resilience required to navigate the challenges of existence. These goddesses challenge traditional perceptions of femininity, illustrating that the divine feminine encompasses a broad spectrum of attributes—nurturing and fierce, wise and powerful, loving and protective.

These goddesses exemplify the divine feminine through their multifaceted roles, connecting the spiritual with the earthly, the nurturing with the warrior, and the wise with the transformative. They remain powerful symbols of the inherent strength and complexity found in femininity, offering a rich legacy that continues to inspire and resonate in contemporary cultures.

These ancient cultures frequently held feminine deities in extraordinarily high regard, recognizing their remarkable ability to govern the forces of both chaos and harmony. This recognition reflects the profound duality that is inherent in women's lived experiences throughout history. The deep reverence for the feminine divine not only provided women with a significant sense of agency but also fostered a strong, enduring connection to the sacred. This connection encouraged community practices that honored, celebrated, and elevated their indispensable roles within society, reinforcing their importance in various social structures.

As we delve into the intricate narratives of these ancient cultures and explore their rich tapestry, we uncover the deep and enduring roots of feminine spirituality. These roots continue to resonate powerfully in modern times, shaping contemporary understandings of the divine. This ongoing influence inspires a diverse range of contemporary expressions of the divine feminine, highlighting the timelessness and relevance of these age-old beliefs in today's complex world.

The shift from matriarchal to patriarchal systems marked a significant and transformative turning point in the evolution of the sacred feminine. As societies began to prioritize male deities and adopt hierarchical structures, goddess figures were often relegated to the background or distorted into symbols of temptation and chaos. Despite these challenging contexts, women consistently found innovative ways to reclaim their power and the rich traditions associated with the sacred feminine. Through folk practices, secret rituals, and oral traditions, the essence of the goddess endured, providing both solace and strength to women as they navigated a world that often sought to diminish their inherent value and contributions.

In contemporary society, there is a remarkable revival of interest in goddess archetypes and feminine spirituality, which signifies a far-reaching cultural shift toward healing, empowerment, and a much deeper understanding of the self and one's place within the vast universe. Many women are now actively seeking to reconnect with the sacred feminine, immersing themselves in a diverse and rich array of rituals, meditations, and practices that honor their unique experiences, personal histories, and the profound wisdom passed down from their ancestors. This resurgence is not merely a nostalgic return to the past; rather, it represents a profound reconceptualization of feminine power that wholeheartedly embraces diversity, inclusivity, and the vital importance of personal agency in every woman's life.

Women's personal sovereignty and the freedom of self-determination are fundamental concepts central to the pursuit of equality and empowerment. Personal sovereignty refers to a woman's inherent right to govern her own life, make choices about her body, and define her identity without undue external influence. This autonomy is crucial for fostering a sense of agency, allowing women to navigate their own paths in a world that has historically imposed limitations based on gender.

Self-determination encompasses the ability to make decisions that affect one's life, including choices related to education, career, health, and relationships. It is about having the power to define one's own goals and pursue them without societal or institutional barriers. For women, self-determination is not just a personal right but also a collective struggle against systemic oppression, discrimination, and cultural norms that seek to confine them to traditional roles.

The relationship between personal sovereignty and self-determination is evident in various aspects of life. In health care, for example, it relates to whether women have the autonomy to make informed decisions about their reproductive health, access to medical services, and overall well-being. This autonomy is vital in combating harmful practices and policies that undermine women's health and rights.

In the political sphere, women's personal sovereignty is essential for representation and advocacy. When women are empowered to speak for themselves and participate in decision-making processes, they can influence policies that affect their lives and communities. This representation is crucial for creating a more equitable society where women's voices are heard and valued.

Economically, self-determination allows women to pursue careers and financial independence, challenging the stereotypes and barriers that often limit their opportunities. Empowering women economically not only benefits them personally but also strengthens families and communities, leading to broader societal progress.

Culturally, the acknowledgment of women's sovereignty helps to dismantle patriarchal structures that dictate how women should behave and what roles they should play. By celebrating diverse expressions of femininity and challenging restrictive norms, society can foster an environment where women feel free to be themselves.

The fight for women's personal sovereignty and self-determination is about creating a world where all individuals, regardless of gender, can exercise their rights fully and equally. It is a continuous journey that requires solidarity, advocacy, and a commitment to dismantling the barriers that impede women's freedom to choose their own destinies. Empowering women in this way not only enriches their lives but also contributes to the overall health and progress of society as a whole.

By thoughtfully weaving ancient wisdom into contemporary practices, women are not only forging new and transformative paths of healing but also creating a powerful legacy that honors both their unique journeys and the rich, collective experiences of womanhood throughout history. This dynamic movement cultivates a profound sense of community and shared purpose, encouraging women to uplift and support one another as they navigate their spiritual journeys and reclaim their sacred identities with renewed vigor and determination. It serves as a poignant reminder that embracing the sacred feminine not only empowers individuals but also strengthens the vital bonds among women. This interconnectedness weaves a vibrant tapestry, rich with shared stories, struggles, triumphs, and a collective resilience that echoes through generations, forming a compelling narrative of strength and unity.

Such deep connections not only enrich the very fabric of society itself but also foster a greater sense of belonging and solidarity among women. This leads to a more compassionate, inclusive, and understanding world for everyone, regardless of gender. Through this collective effort, women are actively redefining their roles in society, thereby inspiring future generations to embrace their rich heritage and invaluable wisdom. This ensures that the lessons of the past continue to illuminate the paths of those who will follow, guiding them towards a future filled with hope, empowerment, and shared growth. As women come together in this mission, they not only uplift themselves but also inspire a broader cultural shift that recognizes the importance of collaboration and mutual support in creating lasting change. This movement reinforces the idea that when women unite, their collective strength has the power to transform not just individual lives but entire communities, paving the way for a more just and equitable world for all.

The sacred feminine is not merely a relic of history; it is a vibrant, evolving force that continues to shape and influence women's lives today in profound and meaningful ways. As we navigate the intricate layers of our identities and the often burdensome societal expectations imposed upon us, the timeless lessons imparted by various goddess figures can serve as powerful and transformative guides in our journeys of self-discovery. These archetypal figures remind us of our inherent strength and resilience, inspiring us to rise above challenges and adversity. From embodying resilience in the face of hardships to celebrating the unique beauty of our bodies and the sacredness of our diverse experiences, the divine feminine calls upon us to fully embrace our potential and authenticity without reservation or fear.

By digging deeply into the rich historical context and evolution of these archetypes, we can reclaim our narratives, honor our journeys, and empower ourselves and each other in our collective rise as women in the modern world. This process not only fosters a deeper sense of solidarity and strength among us but also encourages a supportive community that uplifts and inspires every woman to stand firmly in her truth and power. As we connect with these powerful symbols, we cultivate a sense of belonging and purpose, reminding us that we are part of a larger tapestry of womanhood that transcends time and space.

The Importance of Honoring the Feminine

The significance of honoring the feminine in our lives is difficult to overemphasize, particularly in a world that frequently diminishes the value of qualities traditionally associated with femininity. By wholeheartedly embracing the sacred feminine, we not only recognize the divine attributes that dwell within us but also cultivate a deep and meaningful sense of balance within the intricate tapestry of existence. This essential act of honoring serves as a powerful reminder that qualities such as intuition, nurturing, creativity, and collaboration are not merely desirable traits but are fundamental to our personal growth, the well-being of our communities, and the overall harmony of society.

In a culture that often praises aggression and competition, the recognition and elevation of the feminine invites a profound and transformative shift toward healing, understanding, and empowerment for all individuals, irrespective of gender. Embracing these essential qualities nurtures an environment where everyone can truly thrive, enriching our shared experiences and paving the way for a more inclusive and compassionate future for all.

By doing this, we lay the groundwork for a world that not only values but actively integrates both masculine and feminine energies. This balance fosters a more harmonious and equitable existence for everyone involved, allowing us to navigate life with greater empathy, connection, and understanding. It is through this conscious acknowledgment and celebration of feminine qualities that we can inspire a collective awakening, encouraging deeper relationships, emotional intelligence, and a genuine sense of community. As we commit to this journey of integration, we empower ourselves and others, creating a ripple effect that enhances the fabric of society and nurtures a legacy of love and respect for generations to come.

Goddess archetypes serve as powerful and evocative symbols of the rich and diverse expressions of femininity that can be found across a wide array of cultures and historical contexts. From the nurturing and motherly qualities embodied by Demeter to the fierce independence and warrior spirit exemplified by Kali, these remarkable figures remind us that femininity is not a singular or monolithic identity but rather a vast and intricate spectrum of attributes, energies, and experiences. Engaging with these archetypes can provide invaluable insights for women at various stages of life as they explore their own identities, leading to a deeper sense of self-awareness, acceptance, and empowerment.

By embodying the characteristics and virtues of these powerful goddesses, women can draw upon their strength, wisdom, and resilience, fostering a profound and transformative connection to their own innate power and potential. This enriching process not only enhances individual empowerment but also honors and celebrates the collective experience of womanhood throughout history. It weaves together a rich tapestry of shared narratives and experiences that resonate across generations and cultures, creating a legacy of strength and inspiration for future generations.

The exploration of these archetypes encourages women to reflect on their personal journeys and the unique challenges they face, allowing them to find solace and guidance in the experiences of these divine figures. As they navigate the complexities of life, the lessons imparted by these goddesses can serve as a source of encouragement and motivation, reinforcing the idea that every woman has the capacity to embody her own form of strength and wisdom. By embracing this journey, women not only cultivate their own identities but also contribute to an ongoing dialogue about femininity that enriches the cultural landscape for all, ensuring that the stories of women continue to be told and celebrated.

Feminine spirituality practices undoubtedly play a pivotal and essential role in honoring, celebrating, and uplifting the sacred feminine within all women. Engaging in a diverse array of rituals, meditations, and sacred ceremonies creates not only meaningful but also transformative spaces for women to reconnect deeply, not only with themselves but also with one another. This connection fosters a profound sense of sisterhood, solidarity, and shared experience among participants, nurturing bonds that can last a lifetime and transcend individual experiences. These practices can vary widely, encompassing everything from something as simple and accessible as a daily gratitude meditation to more elaborate and immersive gatherings, like a full moon celebration, where women come together in unity, shared purpose, and mutual support, enriching their communal spirit.

By intentionally setting aside dedicated time to honor the feminine within themselves, women cultivate a deeper and more enriching relationship with their bodies, emotions, and spirits. This intentional focus allows for significant personal growth and healing across multiple levels, creating a ripple effect that enhances individual well-being and nurtures confidence. Furthermore, this process nurtures a powerful collective energy that empowers all women to thrive, flourish, and reach their fullest potential in their lives and their communities. Through these sacred practices, women can reclaim their power and celebrate the unique journeys they have undertaken, recognizing the value of each story and experience. By doing so, they create a supportive and uplifting community that not only benefits and uplifts everyone involved but also fosters connections that inspire future generations, cultivate a legacy of empowerment, resilience, and shared wisdom. Such practices serve as a vital reminder of the strength found in unity and the beauty of collective experience, illustrating how interconnectedness enhances the journey of every woman while weaving a rich tapestry of empowerment that spans generations

The sacred feminine provides a profoundly rich lens through which we can gain deeper insights into the healing process, both personally and on a larger collective scale. Many women not only carry their own wounds but also bear the burdens of ancestral scars and societal pressures that significantly hinder their growth, authenticity, and overall well-being. By honoring and embracing the sacred feminine, we open up meaningful avenues to explore a wide range of healing techniques that promote self-love, acceptance, and empowerment across all areas of life. This transformative journey often requires us to acknowledge the inherent sacredness of our bodies, recognize the natural rhythms of our cycles, and adopt holistic approaches to health that harmoniously integrate mind, body, and spirit.

Engaging in practices that joyfully celebrate our unique femininity empowers us to reclaim our personal narratives, allowing us to express our true selves more fully. In doing so, we pave the way for a richer and more interconnected collective healing experience. This transformation holds immense potential to change how we see ourselves, redefine our connections with others, and illuminate the vital roles we play in the intricate tapestry of the world around us. By recognizing the interconnectedness of our experiences and the shared nature of our journeys, we not only heal individually but also contribute to a larger collective awakening. This creates a ripple effect that nurtures and uplifts our communities, fostering deeper connections that resonate far beyond our immediate circles. This journey toward embracing the sacred feminine is not just about personal healing; it is about weaving a stronger, more compassionate community that thrives on shared understanding and support

In contemporary contexts, women embody and express the sacred feminine in a multitude of profound and transformative ways, intricately weaving these vital principles into the very fabric of their daily lives and interactions. Whether through passionate activism that boldly challenges deeply entrenched societal norms and injustices, innovative creative expressions that push boundaries and inspire others, or impactful community-building initiatives that foster connection, support, and a rich sense of belonging, modern women are courageously redefining and reshaping what it truly means to honor the feminine essence in today's complex and often turbulent world. By fully embracing their unique journeys, multifaceted experiences, and diverse backgrounds, they significantly contribute to a larger, transformative movement aimed at empowerment, healing, and meaningful societal change that resonates deeply across generations and transcends cultural boundaries.

This collective effort not only empowers individual women but also inspires entire communities to engage in meaningful dialogues that foster understanding, empathy, and solidarity. Such interactions pave the way for a more inclusive and equitable future where every voice is valued. In this way, women stand as vital agents of change, illuminating the path toward a world that not only celebrates but also deeply honors the sacred feminine in all its diverse and beautiful forms. Their resilience and creativity become a beacon of hope, guiding society toward a deeper appreciation of the interconnectedness of all beings and the importance of nurturing a compassionate and equitable world for future generations.

As we gather together to joyfully celebrate the sacred feminine, we begin to deeply recognize that honoring this vital aspect of our being is not only essential for personal fulfillment and growth but is also crucial for fostering a more compassionate, harmonious, and balanced world. In such an enriched and vibrant world, the voices of all women are not merely heard but are profoundly valued and respected, allowing for a rich tapestry of diverse perspectives to emerge, thrive, and flourish. Through this collective endeavor, we can rise together, fully embracing the profound strength, wisdom, and beauty of the feminine in all its diverse forms and manifestations. By doing so, we actively contribute to creating a more inclusive and thriving society that benefits everyone, paving the way for future generations to continue this vital work, legacy, and mission with unwavering passion and purpose.

Let us find sisterhood in this sacred journey, recognizing the interconnectedness of our experiences, uplifting one another, and creating spaces where the feminine spirit can shine brightly and radiate its transformative energy. In our shared commitment, we cultivate an environment where every voice matters, fostering a world where collaboration, empathy, and understanding flourish.

This, in turn, leads to a future filled with hope and possibility for all, inspiring us to engage in meaningful dialogue and action that honors the essence of the feminine. Together, we forge connections that transcend boundaries, weaving a stronger fabric of community and support for one another. As we honor the sacred feminine, we lay the groundwork for a world that not only values diversity but celebrates it, ensuring that the wisdom and insight of women are integral to the progress of humanity as a whole. This effort ensures that the rich heritage of the sacred feminine is cherished, nurtured, and continuously passed down through the ages, inspiring countless individuals to join in this essential quest for balance, understanding, and acceptance in our ever-evolving world. As we reinforce the idea that the sacred feminine is a powerful force for unity and transformation, we recognize its immense potential to lead us toward a more equitable and just society, where every voice matters, and every contribution counts.

This collective movement fosters a brighter future for all, one where the sacred feminine is not just acknowledged but celebrated and revered as a cornerstone of human experience and connection, enriching our lives and strengthening our communities. In this way, we create a legacy that honors the past while inspiring hope for the future, ensuring that the sacred feminine continues to illuminate our paths forward.

Goddess Archetypes

The Mother, Queen of Nurturing and Creation

The archetype of the Mother stands as a timeless and universal figure that transcends cultural boundaries, resonating profoundly within the hearts of women from a multitude of backgrounds and experiences across all walks of life. She embodies not only the essence of nurturing, creation, and unconditional love but also serves as a powerful reminder of the inherent strength and potential that each woman harbors within herself. In the realm of the sacred feminine, the Mother transcends her traditional role as a biological parent; she emerges as a profound force of life and sustenance, acting as a wellspring of creativity, healing, and transformative energy.

By embracing this archetype, women can reconnect with their intrinsic ability to nurture themselves, care for others, and cultivate a deeper, more meaningful relationship with the world around them. This connection fosters a greater sense of community, belonging, and empowerment, enabling women to uplift one another and create supportive networks that celebrate their shared experiences, wisdom, and unique journeys. Indeed, the archetype of the Mother serves as an enduring source of inspiration, urging women to recognize their collective strength and the immense power that lies within them. This archetype encourages a harmonious bond that not only enriches their lives but also profoundly impacts the lives of those they touch. By cultivating this nurturing spirit, women create a legacy of empowerment and love that spans generations, nurturing future generations with the same values of compassion, resilience, and support. In doing so, they forge connections that deepen their understanding of themselves and each other, allowing them to thrive in a world that often challenges their innate abilities. As they embrace the Mother within, women become a transformative force in their communities, championing the importance of solidarity, shared wisdom, and the beauty of their unique journeys.

Throughout history, various goddess figures have profoundly embodied the Mother archetype, each reflecting a unique set of attributes that resonate deeply with distinct cultural contexts and societal values. From the ancient Egyptian goddess Isis, who symbolizes not only the profound aspects of motherhood and fertility but also the deep mysteries of magic, healing, and wisdom, to the Hindu goddess Durga, a fierce protector who embodies extraordinary strength and resilience as she nurtures her children while bravely confronting formidable forces of darkness and evil, these powerful figures offer rich narratives and profound insights into the multifaceted female experience. They serve as vital touchstones through which women can explore their own diverse experiences of motherhood, creation, and empowerment in deeply meaningful and transformative ways that resonate across time and geography. By questing through these myths and legends, we can discover invaluable lessons about resilience, compassion, and the transformative power of love that transcends generations and cultural boundaries. These timeless stories provide essential guidance and inspiration, encouraging us to reflect thoughtfully on contemporary life and the myriad challenges we face today. They remind us of the enduring strength and unwavering spirit of the feminine essence that has shaped humanity throughout the ages, inviting us to honor and celebrate the contributions of women throughout history and the ongoing journey of empowerment that continues to unfold in our present day.

Feminine spirituality practices frequently center around rituals that honor and celebrate the nurturing energy of the Mother, a force that is not only immensely powerful but also profoundly transformative in its essence. These rituals, while they may appear simple in their execution, hold deep significance and can encompass a richly diverse array of activities that resonate profoundly with our innermost selves and reflect our personal experiences. They may include the thoughtful creation of altars adorned with meaningful symbols of motherhood, such as vibrant flowers that celebrate the essence of life, inspiring images that evoke strength and resilience, and cherished tokens that poignantly reflect our unique personal journeys and stories. Engaging in meditative practices that focus on fostering self-love, cultivating acceptance, and nurturing compassion is essential for our emotional well-being.

Equally important is our active participation in community gatherings that joyfully celebrate the natural cycles of life. These celebrations often highlight the changing seasons and the various phases of the moon, allowing us to connect more profoundly with nature's rhythms and the heartbeat of the universe itself. By consciously incorporating these enriching practices into our daily lives and routines, we awaken the nurturing spirit that resides within each of us. This awakening reinforces our connection to the sacred feminine energy that envelops us all, reminding us of our shared heritage and the collective strength we possess. Such practices empower us to cultivate a deeper understanding of our own bodies, our inherent capacity for creation, and our ability to nurture ourselves and others in a multitude of meaningful ways. This creation can manifest in various forms—whether through the birthing of children, engaging in artistic expressions that authentically reflect our inner truths, or fostering and nurturing meaningful relationships with those who surround us.

These rituals not only connect us to our personal journeys but also to a broader communal experience of the sacred feminine. They foster a profound sense of belonging and unity among women and allies alike. In doing so, we create a supportive network that enriches our lives and uplifts our spirits, allowing us to thrive collectively and individually in this sacred journey of existence. By embracing these practices, we not only celebrate our individuality but also honor the collective experience that binds us in our shared quest for understanding and fulfillment. Through shared rituals, we deepen our connection with one another, fostering an environment where love, support, and growth can flourish. These moments of collective celebration remind us that we are not alone in our journeys; we are part of a vibrant tapestry woven from the threads of our stories, experiences, and aspirations. This interconnectedness enhances our ability to navigate life's challenges with resilience, drawing strength from the community that uplifts us. Thus, as we engage in these sacred practices, we not only honor the multiplicity of our experiences but also contribute to a more profound, collective understanding of the divine feminine that exists within and around us.

Healing and empowerment are not merely vital themes; they represent deeply interconnected concepts that resonate profoundly with the Mother archetype across a rich tapestry of cultural narratives. Throughout various spiritual traditions, the Mother is venerated as an extraordinary healer, embodying essential qualities such as compassion, nurturing, and the profound capacity for forgiveness. Women have the unique opportunity to tap into this nurturing energy, enabling them to confront and heal both personal and collective wounds. In doing so, they foster a deep sense of empowerment that emerges from a genuine understanding and acceptance of their individual experiences and the shared experiences of their communities.

Numerous techniques, including journaling, guided visualization, and group therapy, can be effectively employed to explore the multifaceted impact of motherhood—capturing both its uplifting joys and its challenging trials—on our lives. By actively engaging with these transformative practices, we not only honor our unique journeys as mothers or daughters, but we also contribute meaningfully to the healing of the wider community around us. This active engagement reinforces the interconnectedness of our experiences and highlights the transformative power inherent in shared narratives. It serves as a powerful reminder that our collective stories can foster resilience, promote understanding, and inspire hope in the face of adversity.

In the modern age, women can embody the sacred feminine and the Mother archetype in an astonishing array of diverse and deeply meaningful ways that resonate powerfully across various spheres of life. This embodiment manifests in passionate activism that fervently champions social justice and equity, innovative creative expressions that inspire profound societal change, and nurturing, supportive relationships that uplift and empower others. The essence of the Mother can be uniquely and beautifully expressed in each woman's individual journey and experiences, illustrating the myriad paths that lead to personal fulfillment and community impact. By advocating for necessary comforts such as self-care, mental health awareness, and body positivity, women not only create inclusive and welcoming spaces but also forge vibrant communities that honor the sacred feminine. They recognize its profound connection to overall well-being and empowerment, fostering environments where individuals can truly thrive.

As we celebrate these varied and rich expressions of the Mother archetype, we come to understand that the Mother within each of us transcends traditional notions of motherhood; she emerges as a dynamic and transformative force that encourages personal growth, profound healing, and the joyful celebration of life in all its myriad forms and complexities. This multifaceted representation of the Mother archetype invites us to explore the richness of our identities in greater depth and to embrace the diverse and enriching roles we play in nurturing ourselves and others in this interconnected world. Engaging in these practices fosters a sense of belonging and shared purpose among us all, reminding us that the spirit of the Mother can manifest in countless ways. It weaves a vibrant tapestry of connection and support that uplifts both individuals and communities alike. Through these collective efforts, we not only honor the sacred feminine but also contribute to a more compassionate, equitable, and just society for everyone. In doing so, we ensure that the values of empathy, understanding, and unwavering support resonate widely throughout our shared human experience, enriching our lives and strengthening the bonds that unite us in our common humanity. Together, we can cultivate nurturing environments where these essential values flourish, enabling future generations to thrive in a world that celebrates the sacred feminine as a vital force for positive change and transformation. By embracing this powerful journey, we can inspire one another and create a lasting legacy of compassion and resilience that will resonate for years to come. We can also inspire a broader movement that not only elevates the voices of women but also recognizes the strengths inherent in every individual, fostering a culture of mutual respect and understanding. As we continue this journey, we empower ourselves and others, building bridges that connect us all in our shared quest for a more inclusive and supportive world.

The Warrior, Champion of Strength and Protection

In the intricate tapestry of feminine archetypes, the Warrior emerges as a striking and powerful symbol of strength, resilience, and protection. Embodying both the fierce and nurturing aspects of the sacred feminine, the Warrior transcends mere physical prowess or martial skill; she embodies a deeper, more profound energy that empowers women to stand resolute in their convictions while safeguarding not only themselves but also their communities and loved ones. Across various cultures and civilizations, goddesses such as Durga, Athena, and Sekhmet serve as dynamic embodiments of this archetype, each illustrating the diverse and multifaceted ways that strength and protection can manifest in a woman's life.

As we embark on a transformative journey to explore the Warrior within ourselves, we begin to gain valuable insights into how this fierce energy can be harnessed not only for healing and personal empowerment but also for nurturing our inner selves and those around us. This exploration leads to a more profound connection with our authentic identities, enhancing our understanding of the world and enriching our relationships with others. Embracing the Warrior archetype allows us to recognize our own strength and resilience, inspiring us to rise above challenges and advocate for ourselves and those we care about. In doing so, we learn to navigate life's complexities with confidence and grace, fostering a sense of unity and support within our communities. The Warrior within us serves as a reminder that true power lies in compassion, courage, and the unwavering commitment to protect and uplift ourselves and each other.

The Warrior's strength is profoundly rooted in her extraordinary ability to confront challenges head-on, embodying an unwavering determination and resilience that is both admirable and deeply inspiring. This does not imply aggression or violence; rather, it serves as a powerful invitation for women to wholeheartedly embrace courage and resilience, especially when faced with adversity in its many forms.

In the increasingly complex and multifaceted landscape of modern life, women often find themselves navigating a myriad of societal pressures, personal struggles, and intricate relationships that can feel overwhelming and isolating. These experiences can lead to moments of doubt and uncertainty, shaking their sense of self and making it difficult to maintain confidence in their abilities and choices. By embracing the Warrior archetype, women can tap into their unique strengths and gifts, fostering a profound sense of empowerment that encourages them to advocate fiercely not only for themselves but also for others in their communities. This advocacy can create a supportive network of solidarity that uplifts everyone involved, reinforcing the idea that strength is best shared and nurtured collectively, creating a sense of unity and shared purpose that resonates throughout the entire community.

Engaging in rituals that honor this vital aspect of the sacred feminine can encompass a diverse range of physical practices, including martial arts, yoga, dance, or even hiking and nature walks, all of which cultivate not only physical strength but also mental clarity and emotional stability. These enriching practices serve to help women connect with their inner power, enabling them to face life's numerous obstacles with confidence, grace, and an unshakeable sense of purpose that resonates deeply within their souls. By nurturing this Warrior spirit, women can inspire themselves and others to rise above challenges, reinforcing the belief that they are not only capable of overcoming obstacles but also of achieving greatness in all facets of their lives. This journey of empowerment sets a powerful example for future generations, illustrating that resilience and strength can transcend boundaries and empower women to create a lasting impact in the world around them. In doing so, they foster an environment where future leaders can emerge, equipped with the courage and tenacity to navigate their own paths with confidence and grace. It is this collective journey, rooted in shared experiences and mutual support, that solidifies the bonds among women and inspires a movement toward greater equality and understanding, contributing to a more just and compassionate society for all.

Protection stands as not only an essential and vital facet of the Warrior archetype but also embodies a profound and unwavering commitment to safeguarding oneself while nurturing others throughout life's journey. This protective energy extends far beyond merely guarding against external threats; it encompasses the equally significant nurturing of inner peace and self-love, both of which serve as foundational elements for personal growth and holistic development. Women are encouraged to actively cultivate safe spaces within their lives—be it through the establishment of supportive friendships, the practice of sacred rituals, or the creation of personal retreats—where they can authentically connect with their true selves and engage in deep exploration of their innermost thoughts and feelings. This crucial aspect of the Warrior not only emphasizes the importance of individual empowerment but also aligns seamlessly with the collective healing processes often vital within women's communities. Women frequently find themselves called to protect and uplift one another, fostering an environment in which they come to recognize that their true strength lies in unity and mutual support. Through the bonds of community, we can share our stories and wisdom, validate our diverse experiences, and cultivate a culture of unwavering support that reinforces our shared strength and resilience. This collective effort creates a nurturing environment where we can all thrive together, celebrating each other's victories, offering encouragement during trying times, and navigating challenges side by side. In doing so, we enrich our lives and the lives of those around us, creating an enduring legacy of love, strength, and empowerment that transcends individual experiences and fosters lasting connections. By embracing these principles, we not only honor the Warrior within but also contribute to a larger tapestry of support and empowerment that uplifts everyone in our community.

In the rich and diverse realm of mythology, the Warrior archetype emerges as a compelling and multifaceted figure who beautifully transcends traditional gender roles, powerfully showcasing the dynamic balance between strength and femininity. Myths surrounding formidable goddesses such as Artemis, who fearlessly roams the vast wilderness with her bow and arrows, or Sekhmet, the fierce protector of the Egyptian pantheon, vividly illustrate how these divine figures wield their considerable power not only to protect the vulnerable but also to uphold justice and moral integrity. By seeking out these tales, modern women can glean invaluable insights into how they too can embody the Warrior spirit in their own lives. They are encouraged to draw from the rich wisdom embedded in these ancient stories, using the lessons learned to inspire their own transformative journeys of empowerment, resilience, and self-discovery.

This process not only fosters profound personal growth but also serves as a powerful reminder of the strength inherent in embracing both femininity and warrior-like valor. Through this exploration, women can forge a powerful and lasting connection with the archetype, discovering immense strength in their femininity while simultaneously embracing and celebrating their warrior attributes. In doing so, they can navigate the complexities of modern life with confidence and purpose, transforming challenges into valuable opportunities for growth and empowerment. Furthermore, this journey is not just about individual transformation; it also encourages a collective consciousness among women, creating a supportive community that uplifts and inspires one another. This path leads to a more fulfilled and empowered existence, where the harmonious integration of strength and compassion paves the way for a brighter future. By embodying the Warrior spirit, women can become catalysts for change, influencing not only their own lives but also the lives of those around them. The enduring legacy of these mythological figures serves as a guiding light, illuminating the path toward empowerment and self-actualization.

As women continue to reclaim their narratives and wholeheartedly embrace the sacred feminine in contemporary contexts, the Warrior archetype emerges as an incredibly powerful guiding force, illuminating the path toward empowerment and profound self-discovery.

In a world that often seeks to diminish women's voices and contributions, embodying the Warrior means standing tall, confidently asserting one's presence with unwavering determination, and creating space for both vulnerability and strength. This essential duality allows women to navigate the complexities of life with the ability to be fierce yet compassionate, brave yet tender, creating a holistic sense of self that is both inspiring and transformative. By integrating a diverse array of practices that honor this archetype—whether through meditation, visualization, creative expression, or active community involvement—women can cultivate the resilience needed to navigate their lives with unwavering confidence, grace, and authenticity. This resilience not only enhances personal growth but also fosters a supportive network among women, encouraging collaboration and solidarity.

In embracing this journey, women honor their own paths while making significant contributions to a collective awakening of the sacred feminine. This collective movement generates a ripple effect that empowers not only themselves but also future generations, fostering an environment where women's voices are amplified and celebrated in all their rich diversity. Through this shared commitment to uplift one another, women can inspire each other to embrace their unique strengths and build a lasting legacy of strength, empowerment, and sisterhood that will resonate for years to come. This ensures that future generations inherit a world brimming with possibilities, respect for the feminine spirit, and a profound appreciation for the diverse experiences of women. By standing together in solidarity, they create a powerful force for change, paving the way for a more inclusive and equitable future.

The Wise Woman, Teacher of Knowledge and Intuition

The archetype of the Wise Woman embodies the profound knowledge and intuition that emerge from the depths of feminine experience, serving as a radiant beacon of wisdom and understanding in a world that often overlooks and undervalues such invaluable qualities. This revered figure is celebrated across a multitude of cultures and mythologies worldwide, representing not only the rich culmination of life lessons learned over a lifetime but also the remarkable ability to weave together ancient wisdom from the past with fresh insights and foresight for the future.

In today's fast-paced and often chaotic world, where the relentless pursuit of external validation frequently overshadows our inner truth and authentic selves, the Wise Woman beckons us to reconnect with our inherent knowing and to trust the intuitive guidance that resides deep within each of us. She stands as a powerful reminder that true wisdom transcends mere intellectual understanding; it is also deeply intuitive, cultivated through rich experiences, thoughtful reflection, and a profound connection to the natural rhythms of nature and the universe that surrounds us. By embracing this archetype, we unlock the immense potential to navigate the intricate complexities of life with grace, clarity, and confidence, honoring both our past experiences and our future aspirations. In doing so, we not only honor the enduring legacy of the Wise Woman but also empower ourselves to become more attuned to the subtle whispers of wisdom that guide us on our journeys through life, nurturing our spirits and illuminating our paths in ways that inspire and uplift.

This connection to the Wise Woman encourages us to cultivate a deeper understanding of ourselves and the world, fostering resilience and inner strength as we navigate the myriad challenges and opportunities that life presents. It invites us to celebrate the interconnectedness of all experiences, recognizing that each moment contributes to our growth and understanding. Through this lens, we can appreciate the unique insights that arise from our personal journeys, allowing us to embrace our individuality while finding strength in our shared humanity. The Wise Woman archetype not only enriches our understanding of wisdom but also empowers us to become conduits of that wisdom, inspiring others to embark on their own transformative journeys towards self-discovery and enlightenment. In recognizing the essence of the Wise Woman within us, we are reminded of the importance of nurturing our intuition and honoring the life lessons we have gathered. Each experience shapes us and adds depth to our understanding, urging us to listen closely to the inner voice that often speaks in whispers. This inner dialogue, when cultivated, leads to a profound sense of clarity and purpose, guiding us through the complexities of our existence. As we embrace this archetype, we not only illuminate our own paths but also create a ripple effect, encouraging those around us to seek their own truths and to honor the wisdom that lies within. Thus, the Wise Woman serves as both a mentor and a muse, inviting us to delve deeper into the wellspring of knowledge that resides in each of us, enriching our lives and the lives of those we touch.

Across a world of diverse cultures and traditions, the archetype of the Wise Woman emerges under a multitude of names and titles, each imbued with its own unique significance and meaning. Whether she is honored as the Crone in Celtic folklore, regarded as the Grandmother in various Indigenous spiritualities, or recognized as the Shaman in numerous spiritual practices and beliefs, her essence remains an enduring and powerful constant throughout time. Each of these representations highlights her essential and transformative role as a keeper of ancient wisdom, a compassionate healer, and a wise guide for those earnestly seeking her invaluable counsel. These remarkable women often find themselves standing at the crossroads of life, uniquely gifted with the ability to see beyond superficial appearances and delve deeply into the very heart of matters, illuminating profound truths that might otherwise remain concealed from view.

The exploration and understanding of these powerful archetypal figures not only allow us to draw inspiration from their rich stories but also provide invaluable lessons that resonate across time and cultures. This exploration encourages us to recognize that we, too, possess the innate capacity to access the divine wisdom that resides within ourselves, inviting us to embark on a transformative journey of self-discovery. Engaging in this inner exploration fosters personal growth, cultivates a deeper understanding of ourselves and others, and enhances our sense of purpose as we navigate our unique journeys through the intricate complexities of existence. In doing so, we honor the legacy and contributions of these Wise Women while empowering ourselves to seek truth and wisdom in our own lives. By embracing this journey, we not only pay tribute to their wisdom but also unlock the potential for profound transformation within ourselves, allowing their teachings to guide us through the challenges and mysteries of our own paths

Embracing the Wise Woman archetype encourages us to actively engage in practices that deeply honor our intuition and amplify our inner voice, guiding us on a transformative journey of self-discovery and personal growth. Rituals such as journaling, meditation, and nature walks not only facilitate a greater understanding of our own life experiences but also help us uncover the profound messages they carry, revealing insights that might otherwise remain hidden and unexamined.

By intentionally creating sacred spaces within our lives, we grant ourselves the invaluable freedom to explore our thoughts and feelings without any judgment or fear of criticism from ourselves or others. This nurturing environment not only fosters the growth of our intuitive abilities but also empowers us to make decisions that are truly aligned with our authentic selves. In doing so, we enable ourselves to live more fully and authentically, rather than merely conforming to societal expectations that may not resonate with our true essence. This journey encourages a deeper connection to our inner wisdom, allowing us to navigate life with clarity, purpose, and a profound sense of fulfillment. By fully embracing the Wise Woman archetype, we embark on a path that celebrates our unique insights and perspectives, cultivating a sense of empowerment that encourages us to trust ourselves and our instincts. The rituals we engage in serve as powerful tools for reflection and growth, enabling us to peel back the layers of our experiences and uncover the hidden truths within. As we carve out sacred spaces in our busy lives, we create opportunities for introspection and self-care, nurturing our souls and fostering a sense of peace. This holistic approach not only enriches our understanding of ourselves but also enhances our ability to connect with others in meaningful ways. In essence, this journey becomes a celebration of our true selves, guiding us toward a life filled with authenticity, joy, and purpose.

The journey of the Wise Woman profoundly emphasizes the critical importance of healing—both on a deeply personal level and within our broader collective community. As we delve deep into our intuitive wisdom, we become increasingly attuned to the emotional and physical wounds we carry, alongside the healing that is not only essential for our growth but also vital for our overall well-being. This journey is not merely a personal endeavor; it is a shared experience that connects us to a much larger narrative, one that has been unfolding through generations and across diverse cultures. Through this transformative process, we come to recognize the profound interconnectedness of our individual experiences with those of countless other women throughout history, creating a rich and intricate tapestry woven from shared struggles, resilience, and triumphs that span across time and space.

By openly sharing our stories, experiences, and insights, and by actively supporting one another in our journeys, we forge a powerful and resilient network of healing that honors, uplifts, and celebrates the sacred feminine in all its diverse forms. This collective empowerment not only allows us to rise together in solidarity but also transforms our pain into profound strength, turning our accumulated wisdom into meaningful action that can inspire transformative change in our communities and beyond. In doing so, we nurture future generations, ensuring that the legacy of healing continues to thrive and that women feel empowered to embrace their own unique journeys. This fosters a culture of compassion, understanding, and solidarity that transcends the barriers of time and space. Through this interconnected web of support, we can break the cycles of silence and isolation, weaving a future where healing is a shared and celebrated experience for all. In doing so, we create an enduring legacy for those who come after us, one that encourages a journey of empowerment, connection, and unity among women everywhere. Each of us contributes to this legacy, enriching our collective narrative as we embrace our stories not just as isolated events, but as vital threads in a larger fabric of shared experience. This interconnectedness deepens our understanding of one another and reinforces our commitment to fostering a community where every woman feels valued, seen, and heard. Together, we embark on a path of healing that not only honors our past but also illuminates the way forward, creating a future that is bright with possibility and hope.

In today's rapidly evolving world, the Wise Woman archetype holds increasingly vital significance as women navigate the intricate complexities of modern life. Many women are actively reclaiming their personal power by tapping into their intuition and self-awareness while creating supportive communities that honor and elevate the wisdom of the feminine spirit. Through a diverse array of workshops, circles, retreats, and online platforms, women are discovering their voices, sharing their unique perspectives, and forming meaningful connections that foster growth, solidarity, and empowerment.

By taking on the essence of the Wise Woman, we not only honor our individuality but also pave the way for future generations to access their own inner wisdom, strength, and resilience. This transformative journey allows us to joyfully celebrate the sacred feminine in all its myriad forms, recognizing that the path to wisdom is as important and enriching as the wisdom itself. Each step we take not only enriches our lives but also contributes to a broader awakening and empowerment among women everywhere, fostering a collective consciousness that nurtures creativity, compassion, and resilience in the face of life's challenges. Together, we are building a powerful legacy that inspires and uplifts, ensuring that the wisdom of the Wise Woman continues to resonate and thrive for generations to come. This empowers women to embrace their potential and share their gifts with the world, creating ripples of change that extend beyond ourselves. As we unite in this sacred journey, we cultivate a profound sense of belonging and purpose, reminding each other of the strength found in our shared experiences. We invite all women to join in this celebration of the feminine spirit, where every voice matters and every story adds to the rich tapestry of our collective wisdom. Through this commitment to growth and connection, we can transform not only our lives but also the world around us, leaving a lasting impact for those who will follow in our footsteps.

The Lover, Muse of Passion and Sensuality

The archetype of the Lover embodies the profound essence of passion and sensuality, inviting us to delve deeply into the intricate layers of our desires and the exquisite beauty of our physical existence. Across various cultures, goddesses associated with love and sensuality—such as Aphrodite, Freya, and Oshun—serve as powerful reminders that our bodies are not mere vessels but rather sacred spaces through which we experience the richness of the world around us. This vital connection to the divine feminine encourages us to fully embrace our sensual selves, celebrating and honoring the myriad pleasures of both the body and the heart. In a society often steeped in shame and misunderstanding regarding sexuality and desire, the Lover archetype emerges as a liberating force, guiding us to reclaim our passion as a fundamental and enriching aspect of our spiritual journey. By recognizing and embracing this archetype, we can foster a deeper understanding of ourselves and cultivate a more profound appreciation for the love and connection that permeate our lives. The Lover invites us to explore the full spectrum of our emotions, urging us to connect not only with ourselves but also with others in meaningful ways. Embracing our sensuality is not merely about physical pleasure; it is a holistic experience that encompasses emotional intimacy and spiritual growth. Through this journey, we learn to celebrate the joy of being alive, allowing our hearts to open and our spirits to soar. In doing so, we create spaces for authentic connections and experiences that enrich our existence, reminding us that love, in all its forms, is a vital and transformative force in our lives.

Engaging with the Lover invites us to fully immerse ourselves in rituals that not only celebrate our sensuality but also deepen our connection to the divine. These rituals can take many forms, whether it's through the expressive movements of dance, the creative flow of art, or the calming practice of meditation. Each of these practices offers us the opportunity to craft sacred spaces that honor our bodies and awaken our senses in profoundly transformative ways. Imagine the powerful experience of a ritual bath, infused with fragrant oils that evoke the very essence of nature itself. Picture the warm water enveloping you like a loving embrace, cocooning you in warmth and comfort. As you take the time to immerse yourself in this soothing environment, visualize the water gently washing away any lingering feelings of guilt, shame, or inadequacy that may hinder your ability to fully embrace and enjoy your body. This practice nurtures not only our physical selves but also opens the door to deeper emotional healing and self-discovery. It creates a sacred opportunity for us to connect with the divine feminine within, fostering a profound sense of acceptance for the sacred nature of our desires while encouraging us to revel in the beauty of our unique experiences. By engaging in these rituals, we not only honor ourselves but also cultivate a profound sense of gratitude for our bodies and the myriad joys they bring us. Through this process, we learn to celebrate every facet of our being, allowing ourselves to flourish in the fullness of our existence.

The Lover's story transcends being merely a tale of passion; it evolves into a profoundly empowering narrative of liberation and self-discovery that resonates deeply within us all, echoing the universal journey towards authenticity. By wholeheartedly embracing our sensuality, we reclaim our inherent power, coming to the realization that our desires are not simply facets of ourselves to be concealed or suppressed; rather, they are vital expressions of our true essence—core elements that shape our identity and influence our journeys. Instead of hiding these desires away, they deserve to be celebrated as essential components of our divine nature, integral to our identity and overall well-being.

In the contemporary landscape, women are increasingly uncovering a wealth of diverse avenues through which to express this empowerment and freedom, leading to a vibrant renaissance of self-acceptance and authenticity that not only inspires individuals but also uplifts entire communities across the globe. This enriching exploration encompasses dynamic body positivity movements that boldly challenge and redefine deeply entrenched societal norms, transformative sexual reclamation workshops that fuel personal growth and exploration, as well as engaging in open, honest conversations that delve into their unique experiences and journeys. Such dialogues create spaces where voices can rise in unison, fostering solidarity and connection among women from all walks of life, contributing to a more inclusive and supportive environment for everyone.

Body image and body positivity are profoundly intertwined with the concept of the sacred feminine, which honors and celebrates the inherent beauty and strength found in all bodies, regardless of shape, size, or appearance. In a society often fixated on unrealistic and narrow beauty standards, embracing body positivity emerges as a powerful and transformative movement that encourages individuals to appreciate their unique forms while rejecting harmful ideals that can lead to insecurity, self-doubt, and mental health challenges. The sacred feminine manifests as certain universal qualities such as nurturing, intuition, compassion, and acceptance, inviting individuals to honor their bodies as sacred vessels deserving of love, respect, and care. This holistic perspective fosters a deeper connection to oneself, encouraging profound self-acceptance and appreciation for the incredible diversity of femininity that exists in the world around us. By acknowledging and celebrating the sacred feminine, we can cultivate a culture that genuinely values authenticity, empowerment, and self-expression, allowing everyone to feel confident, beautiful, and worthy in their own skin. Such an approach not only enriches personal lives but also contributes to creating a more inclusive and supportive community where all individuals can thrive, flourish, and be celebrated for who they truly are. Embracing this philosophy paves the way for a collective awakening to the beauty in diversity, fostering a sense of belonging and unity that empowers everyone to shine in their individuality. It encourages us to recognize that every person's journey is valid, and by uplifting one another, we can collectively dismantle the damaging narratives that have long dictated our perceptions of beauty. By nurturing a space where every body is honored and valued, we can inspire a movement that transcends superficial standards, fostering genuine connection and understanding among all people. Commitment to body positivity and the sacred feminine can lead to a profound societal shift, one where love and acceptance become the guiding principles in our interactions with ourselves and each other.

Sexual reclamation, intricately interwoven with the profound and multifaceted concept of the sacred feminine, represents a transformative and deeply enriching journey that encourages individuals to fully embrace and honor their sexuality as a potent source of empowerment, self-discovery, and a profound connection to the divine. This complex and enriching process involves reclaiming the body and its innate desires from the restrictive societal narratives that frequently demonize, stigmatize, or shame female sexuality, thereby creating significant barriers to self-acceptance, self-love, and personal agency.

By nurturing a meaningful and profound relationship with the sacred feminine, individuals can reconnect with their inherent wisdom, creativity, and intuition, recognizing that sexuality is not merely a physical experience but a sacred expression of life energy and vitality that flows through us all, connecting us to the universe and to each other. This powerful act of reclamation not only promotes a holistic understanding of pleasure, consent, and self-love but also encourages individuals to celebrate their bodies and desires as sacred vessels of power, authenticity, and self-acceptance. Sexual reclamation emerges as a vital act of healing and liberation, fostering a deeper connection to oneself and to the divine essence within, allowing individuals to navigate their unique journeys with confidence and grace. This enlightening journey lays the groundwork for a more inclusive, respectful, and compassionate dialogue surrounding sexuality, enriching the collective understanding and appreciation of sexual expression and identity in all its diverse forms. It empowers individuals to advocate for their own needs and desires in a world that often seeks to silence or marginalize them. By embracing this journey, individuals contribute to a broader cultural shift that honors and respects the full spectrum of human sexuality, creating a more accepting and supportive environment for all.

By sharing our diverse stories and uplifting one another on this transformative journey, we cultivate a collective narrative that not only honors but also deeply embraces the powerful essence of the sacred feminine. In doing so, we create a rich tapestry of interconnected experiences that beautifully interweaves our lives. This ongoing transformation serves to not only redefine what has historically been perceived as taboo but also reshapes those perceptions into a formidable source of strength, community, and solidarity among women everywhere. It reinforces the empowering idea that we are indeed stronger together in our shared endeavors. Such meaningful connections foster relationships that uplift, inspire, and create a supportive environment where every woman feels fully empowered to express her true self without hesitation. This nurturing space allows for the flourishing of creativity and individuality, leading to a more vibrant, inclusive world—one where every voice is not only valued but celebrated, and where every story matters profoundly. By embracing our journeys together, we pave the way for a future rich in possibility and connection.

Understanding the Lover archetype invites us to delve even deeper into the intricate and multifaceted relationship between the sacred feminine and our bodies, illuminating the profound connections that shape our existence and define our experiences. Our overall health, fertility, and body image are intricately intertwined with our capacity to fully embrace our sensuality and express our true selves in a world that often challenges and undermines these vital connections. By nurturing our bodies with unwavering love, compassion, and profound respect, we can cultivate a more meaningful and enriching bond with our innate wisdom and intuitive guidance, allowing us to flourish in all aspects of our lives, emotionally, spiritually, and physically. Practicing good habits such as yoga, mindful eating, and body meditation not only enables us to tune in to our physical selves but also fosters a deep sense of appreciation for all that our bodies are capable of achieving, both physically and emotionally. This holistic approach to health and well-being encourages us to joyfully celebrate our unique journeys, recognizing that each woman's experience with her body is sacred, worthy of deep reverence, and deserving of honor in its own right. This recognition leads us to a greater understanding of our place in the rich and interconnected tapestry of life, inviting us to embrace our roles as both individuals and as integral parts of a larger community filled with shared experiences, collective wisdom, and mutual support. By acknowledging and nurturing our interconnectedness, we empower ourselves and each other to thrive in harmony with our true selves, creating a space where we can all flourish, grow, and discover the beauty of our shared humanity together.

In the intricate tapestry of the sacred feminine, the Lover archetype beckons us to immerse ourselves in the rich and multifaceted interplay of passion, sensuality, and empowerment that profoundly shapes our lives. It invites us to delve deeply into the depths of our desires and the connections we share with others. As we honor and fully embrace this vital aspect of ourselves, we not only enhance our own experiences but also play a pivotal role in fostering a broader cultural shift that joyfully celebrates the divine feminine in all of its many beautiful forms and manifestations. This celebration encourages a collective awakening to the significance of the sacred feminine within our lives and societies. By thoughtfully integrating the transformative practices and profound teachings associated with the Lover archetype into our daily routines, rituals, and interactions, we can create a welcoming and nurturing sanctuary where passion and sensuality can thrive and flourish. This environment allows us to express our innermost selves with confidence and without hesitation, encouraging authenticity in our relationships. This journey serves as a powerful reminder to ourselves and to one another that the sacred feminine is an extraordinary and dynamic force—one that not only deserves to be wholeheartedly embraced and celebrated but also fully lived and expressed in all its beauty, richness, and complexity. In doing so, we nurture a deeper connection with ourselves and the world around us, enriching our collective experience while inspiring others to embark on their own transformative journeys of discovery and acceptance. By sharing this journey, we create a ripple effect that enhances the appreciation of the sacred feminine, contributing to a more vibrant and interconnected community that honors the fullness of life.

The Maiden, Lady of Innocence and New Beginnings

The Maiden archetype embodies the vibrant spirit of innocence, exploration, and the promise of new beginnings, serving as a powerful reminder of the beauty inherent in life's early stages. She represents the youthful aspect of the Goddess, inviting us to reconnect with our inner child and the boundless potential that accompanies fresh experiences and uncharted paths. In various cultures, the Maiden is celebrated as a symbol of spring, a season when the earth awakens from the deep slumber of winter, and life begins anew in all its glorious manifestations. This energy of renewal is not merely confined to the rhythms of nature; it resonates profoundly within our own lives, reminding us that each day presents unique opportunities for growth, transformation, and self-discovery that can lead us to richer experiences. In this exploration of the Maiden's essence, we honor her as a guiding force that encourages us to fully embrace our journey, cultivating a deep sense of wonder, curiosity, and limitless possibility in the world around us. She urges us to see every moment as a chance to rediscover joy and creativity, reminding us that life is filled with endless opportunities for exploration and adventure. By tapping into the Maiden's energy, we can reconnect with our dreams and aspirations, allowing ourselves to be inspired by the beauty of our surroundings and the potential that lies ahead. The Maiden invites us to celebrate the present and to approach each day with an open heart and an adventurous spirit, ready to embrace whatever comes our way.

In the rich and multifaceted realm of feminine spirituality, the Maiden archetype extends a heartfelt invitation for us to deeply engage in a diverse array of rituals that celebrate not only our inherent innocence and boundless creativity but also the dynamic emergence of our unique and individual identities. Through simple yet profoundly transformative acts—ranging from journaling our dreams and creating expressive art to immersing ourselves in the breathtaking beauty of nature—we can actively nurture and cultivate the vibrant Maiden within us. These enriching practices empower us to tap into our intuitive wisdom, encouraging us to wholeheartedly embrace the qualities of curiosity, playfulness, and exploration that beautifully define this spirited archetype.

By actively engaging in rituals that honor the Maiden, we not only affirm our unique and individual journeys of self-discovery but also recognize and value the shared experiences of sisterhood that connect us all in a profound way. In this sacred communal space, we uplift, inspire, and support one another as we navigate the diverse and intricate paths of our lives, celebrating the unique and vital contributions each of us brings to the ever-evolving collective narrative that we share. Together, we weave a rich tapestry of experiences that profoundly enriches our understanding and appreciation of the feminine spirit, creating a vibrant and supportive environment for all. This collective journey not only deepens our personal insights but also strengthens the bonds of sisterhood, reminding us that we are never alone as we explore the depths of our being and creativity.

Healing and empowerment are not merely essential; they are also profoundly transformative themes intricately woven into the rich tapestry of the Maiden's journey. She stands as a radiant beacon of inspiration, urging us to confront and courageously release any fears or limiting beliefs that may impede our personal growth and development. By actively engaging in a variety of practices, such as guided meditations, affirmations, and reflective journaling, we can cultivate a deeper and more meaningful connection to our authentic selves. This enlightening process allows us to shed the burdensome layers of societal expectations and self-doubt that often weigh us down and stifle our true potential. Embracing the Maiden's vibrant and dynamic energy equips us with the tools to reclaim our inherent power, enabling us to step boldly into new beginnings and exciting possibilities.

Whether this journey involves pursuing a thrilling new career path, embarking on a creative endeavor that truly ignites our passion, or simply welcoming a new chapter in our personal lives, each step we take is significant and worthy of celebration. This transformative process of healing is not solely an individual journey; it resonates throughout our communities, inspiring a powerful wave of collective empowerment that uplifts everyone around us. It fosters an environment ripe for growth and transformation, where individuals are encouraged to flourish and thrive together. As we navigate this intricate path, we discover that every challenge we face serves as an opportunity for deeper understanding and self-discovery. By embracing vulnerability, we unlock the door to profound insights and connections. The Maiden's journey is a testament to the strength found in unity, as we support one another in overcoming obstacles and celebrating our triumphs. In this shared experience, we create a nurturing space that amplifies our voices, encourages collaboration, and leads to a more vibrant and empowered community. Together, we embark on this extraordinary journey of healing and empowerment, celebrating not just individual achievements, but the collective spirit that binds us all.

Mythology presents a rich and intricate tapestry of stories that beautifully illustrate the attributes of the Maiden across a diverse array of cultures and traditions. Each culture contributes unique and valuable perspectives to this timeless archetype, creating a multifaceted understanding of the Maiden's significance. Figures such as Persephone, who undergoes a profound transformation from innocence to maturity through her remarkable journey in the underworld, and Artemis, the fierce protector of wild spaces and nature, serve as powerful examples of the complex duality and multifaceted nature of the Maiden's journey. These captivating and timeless myths remind us that the path of the Maiden encompasses far more than mere innocence; it requires immense courage to embrace change, confront challenges, and foster meaningful personal growth through adversity and hardship.

By thoroughly studying these profound narratives, we can draw significant parallels to our own lives. We recognize those pivotal moments when we have truly embodied the spirit of the Maiden—whether during times of joy and celebration or while courageously confronting and overcoming life's numerous challenges and obstacles. Engaging with these stories allows us to honor the legacy of the Maiden while also inspiring ourselves to cultivate the same resilience and strength in our own journeys. This engagement serves as a powerful reminder of the human capacity to evolve and adapt. This process empowers us to navigate the complexities of our experiences with grace, determination, and a deeper understanding of ourselves and the world around us. Through this exploration, we not only celebrate the Maiden's journey but also embrace the transformative power of these timeless narratives in shaping our own identities and experiences. As we delve deeper into these mythological tales, we uncover layers of meaning that resonate with our own struggles and triumphs, enriching our understanding of the universal themes that connect us all.

In today's world, the sacred feminine is vividly represented through the numerous and diverse ways in which women embody the spirit of the Maiden in their daily lives. Whether it's the young woman courageously stepping into her first job with determination and excitement, or the devoted mother who lovingly cares for her children while nurturing their dreams and aspirations, the essence of the Maiden thrives in the mindful choices we make and the various paths we boldly pursue with passion and purpose. By celebrating the Maiden within ourselves and acknowledging it in others, we foster a vibrant community that not only honors but also actively engages with the transformative essence of the sacred feminine.

As we navigate life's complexities and challenges, let us remember and cherish the Maiden's invaluable gifts of renewal, innocence, and hope, welcoming new beginnings into our hearts and lives with open arms. In doing so, we honor not just ourselves but also the sacred feminine that connects us all, reminding us of our shared journey and the immense strength we gain from uplifting one another in unity, compassion, and unwavering support. Together, we can create a world that fully embraces and uplifts the sacred feminine, celebrating the myriad of ways it enriches our lives and the lives of those around us.

Let us recognize that the spirit of the Maiden is not confined to a single archetype; it manifests in the resilience of women who advocate for change, in the creativity of artists who express their truths, and in the wisdom of elders who guide the next generation. Each of these expressions contributes to the tapestry of the sacred feminine, weaving a rich narrative that inspires us to pursue our passions and dreams. By elevating these diverse voices and experiences, we enrich our collective understanding and foster an environment where the sacred feminine can flourish. As we stand together, united in our commitment to honor these principles, we not only uplift ourselves but also create a legacy that celebrates the boundless potential of every woman and girl.

Feminine Spirituality Practices

Rituals for Connection and Empowerment

Rituals for Connection and Empowerment are essential practices for women who wish to honor the sacred feminine within themselves and their communities. In the hustle and bustle of modern life, which can often feel overwhelming, these rituals offer a vital sacred pause—a moment to reconnect with our inner selves and the divine feminine energy that surrounds us in every facet of our lives. By drawing on a variety of goddess archetypes from different cultures and traditions, these practices help us access the unique qualities and strengths that resonate with our personal journeys. Whether you resonate with the nurturing essence of Demeter or the fierce independence of Kali, there is a goddess archetype that can guide, inspire, and empower you as you navigate the complexities of contemporary womanhood and the diverse roles we fulfill today.

Engaging in these rituals nurtures a deeper sense of self-awareness and community, fostering connections that are both meaningful and transformative. By invoking the wisdom of these powerful archetypes, we not only reclaim our own stories but also elevate the shared experiences of women around us, weaving a tapestry of strength, resilience, and unity that honors the sacred feminine in all its manifestations. These rituals encourage us to pause, reflect, and embrace the divine within ourselves, empowering us to realize our fullest potential while honoring the rich legacy of those who came before us.

At the very heart of these significant rituals lies a profound intention to nurture deep connections—not only with ourselves but also with the intricate and supportive web of women who have forged the path before us. These remarkable women have established a lineage that is rich in strength, wisdom, and resilience, embodying the spirit of empowerment that has transcended generations. Simple yet transformative practices, such as lighting candles, journaling, or creating altars dedicated to specific goddesses, serve as powerful avenues for honoring our personal journeys, the histories that shape us, and the profound legacies we inherit from those who came before us, reminding us of the strength that lies in our shared experiences.

Gathering together in circles with other women greatly enhances this energy, allowing us to share our stories, wisdom, and support in a nurturing and empowering space that fosters connection and understanding. These communal gatherings create an environment of trust and openness, where we can celebrate our unique differences while also acknowledging and embracing our shared challenges and victories. Through these deep and meaningful connections, we discover empowerment, drawing from the collective strength that embodies the sacred feminine. This shared experience enriches not only our own lives but also the lives of those around us, creating a ripple effect of positivity, encouragement, and solidarity that reverberates through our communities, inspiring us to uplift one another and continue the cycle of strength and support that has been passed down through generations.

Incorporating feminine spirituality practices into our daily lives possesses the extraordinary ability to transform even the most mundane moments into meaningful sacred rituals that resonate with a deeper sense of purpose and connection. For instance, beginning each day with a morning meditation that honors the goddess within ourselves, or engaging in a grounding exercise that connects us to the nurturing earth beneath our feet, can significantly set a powerful and positive tone for the entire day ahead. Such practices not only anchor us but also infuse our daily routines with intention and grace.

Activities such as participating in nature walks, embracing the transformative energies of moon rituals, or expressing our creativity through various forms of art and dance allow us to fully embody the fluidity, grace, and strength of the feminine divine. These enriching practices serve not only as vital reminders of our inherent power but also highlight our remarkable capacity for healing, both on an individual level and within our collective experience. They create a tapestry of connection that enriches our understanding of ourselves and our place in the world. By wholeheartedly embracing these meaningful rituals, we can reclaim, rediscover, and celebrate aspects of ourselves that may have been silenced or forgotten over time. This fosters a profound sense of wholeness, connection, and empowerment that resonates throughout our lives, enhancing our personal journeys and nurturing our relationships with others. As we engage with these practices, we cultivate a deeper appreciation for the sacredness of life and the interwoven threads of our shared experiences.

Healing and empowerment through the lens of the sacred feminine encompass not only the vital act of acknowledging and embracing our bodies in all their diverse and unique forms but also invite us to delve deeper into the profound and intricate connection between our physical selves and the vast universe around us. Engaging in rituals that honor women's health and well-being—such as menstrual celebrations, fertility rites, and a variety of traditional practices—serves not only to reconnect us with our bodies but also with the natural cycles that profoundly define our existence and experiences. By understanding the sacred feminine in relation to our bodies, we foster a compassionate, nurturing relationship with ourselves, fully embracing our unique shapes, diverse experiences, and rich narratives.

This body-centric approach not only honors each of our personal journeys but also acts as a powerful collective movement of reclamation against societal pressures and unrealistic standards that often seek to define and limit us. By celebrating our bodies and sharing our diverse experiences, we not only acknowledge the rich tapestry of individual stories that shape our identities but also create a profound communal space of empowerment that invites all voices to be heard. This sacred space nurtures solidarity, resilience, and strength among women everywhere, inspiring us to uplift one another while embracing our collective wisdom. It fosters an inclusive environment where we advocate for a world in which every woman feels genuinely valued, empowered, and free to express herself authentically in her own unique skin, without fear of judgment or societal constraints. As we embark on this transformative journey together, we recognize the vital importance of mutual support and understanding, effectively creating a powerful network of love and respect that transcends societal limitations and prejudices. Through these shared experiences and meaningful rituals, we not only honor our own personal journeys but also contribute to a larger, more impactful narrative of healing and empowerment for all women. By weaving together the stories of the past and present, we lay the groundwork for a brighter future, one that paves the way for generations to come, inspiring them to embrace their identities and advocate for their rightful place in the world.

This collective endeavor not only strengthens our voices but also amplifies our presence in society, ensuring that we are seen, heard, and valued for who we truly are. Each woman's story adds a vital thread to the narrative of our community, reinforcing the idea that every experience is significant and worthy of recognition. As we come together, let us celebrate the myriad of ways in which we express ourselves and confront challenges, fostering an atmosphere where creativity and individuality flourish. Let us remain committed to promoting an inclusive dialogue that champions equality and respect, paving the way for a future where every woman can thrive and feel empowered in her own journey.

The various rituals we practice can profoundly illuminate the rich and diverse ways in which contemporary women embody and express the sacred feminine in their lives. By intentionally and thoughtfully incorporating these meaningful practices into our daily routines, we weave a complex and vibrant tapestry of empowerment that resonates powerfully across generations and communities. Each ritual serves as a crucial and uplifting reminder of our inherent strength, resilience, and the profound connection to the divine feminine that resides within us all. As we celebrate these vital aspects of ourselves, we not only uplift our spirits but also play a significant role in a broader movement of healing and transformation for all women. This ignites a collective awakening that transcends boundaries, inviting everyone to join in and participate in this sacred journey.

Taking part in these cherished rituals allows us to unite in solidarity, honoring the sacred feminine that vibrantly flows through our lives and the world around us. This shared journey nurtures a deeper sense of community, connection, and purpose, encouraging mutual support, understanding, and compassion in our individual and collective journeys. By engaging in these practices, we cultivate a nurturing space for growth and healing that benefits not just ourselves but also the generations to come, fostering a lasting legacy of strength, empowerment, and inspiration for women everywhere. In doing so, we create a ripple effect that inspires future generations to embrace their own sacred feminine, ensuring that the wisdom and power of these transformative practices continue to thrive and evolve. Furthermore, as we engage in these rituals, we deepen our understanding of our shared histories and experiences, building bridges of empathy and solidarity that strengthen our ties to one another and to the earth itself. This interconnectedness allows us to rise together, amplifying our voices and visions for a world that honors and celebrates the divine feminine in all its forms.

Meditations to Embody the Sacred Feminine

Meditations that focus on embodying the sacred feminine encourage women to forge a profound and authentic connection with the intricate and rich landscape of their inner selves. These transformative practices delve into the deep wisdom found within various goddess archetypes, drawn from a multitude of cultures and historical backgrounds. They guide participants on a multifaceted journey into the essence of femininity, one that is both enlightening and empowering. Each goddess embodies distinct characteristics and qualities—such as intuition, unwavering strength, deep compassion, boundless creativity, and remarkable resilience—inviting us to explore and celebrate the diverse expressions of femininity that exist within us all. By engaging with these divine figures during our meditative practices, we can craft a deeply personal and transformative experience that honors our unique paths, along with the variety of challenges, victories, and insights we encounter along the way. This enriching journey encourages us to recognize and celebrate the immense power of the sacred feminine within our lives, illuminating how it shapes our experiences and perspectives.

By embodying these archetypes in our meditations, we invite their dynamic energies into our daily lives, fostering a meaningful and lasting connection between our inner and outer worlds. This process not only deepens our understanding of our identities as women but also empowers us to navigate our individual paths with unwavering grace, unshakeable confidence, and a steadfast sense of purpose and authenticity that resonates throughout our lives. Embracing the sacred feminine allows us to cultivate a richer, fuller existence, one that honors both our individual journeys and the collective power of womanhood.

To embark on this transformative journey toward self-discovery and empowerment, it is absolutely essential to create a sacred space that resonates deeply with your most cherished intentions and aspirations. This sacred space might manifest as a dedicated corner of your home, thoughtfully adorned with inspiring images of goddesses who uplift and empower you in profound ways. Consider including a carefully selected array of meaningful crystals that hold personal significance for you, as well as natural elements such as vibrant flowers and refreshing water that infuse the area with life and energy, creating a harmonious atmosphere that invites clarity and inspiration.

As you take the time to settle into this sanctuary of peace and inspiration, engage in grounding exercises specifically designed to deepen your connection with the earth beneath you. Visualize your roots extending gracefully from your body into the rich ground below, anchoring you firmly in the present moment and fostering a profound sense of security and belonging that nurtures your spirit. From this place of stability and calm, allow yourself to breathe deeply and intentionally, inviting the essence of the sacred feminine to envelop you in a warm and loving embrace that transcends time and space. With each inhalation, feel the nurturing energy of the Earth Mother flowing through you, along with the fierce protection offered by the warrior goddesses who stand by your side. As these energies merge harmoniously within your being, they empower your spirit in transformative ways that inspire confidence, clarity, and a deeper understanding of your true purpose in this life. Embrace this journey with open arms, knowing that you are supported and guided every step of the way.

Select a goddess who resonates profoundly with your spirit, whether it be the nurturing and abundant essence of Demeter, the fierce and unapologetic independence embodied by Kali, or the profound wisdom and strategic insight that Athena represents. As you begin your meditation, vividly visualize her divine presence standing beside you, enveloping you in her radiant essence and illuminating your surroundings with her light. Allow her powerful attributes to merge seamlessly with your own, filling you with an enriching blend of confidence, love, and clarity that uplifts your entire being and inspires you to fully embrace your limitless potential.

As you immerse yourself in this meditative state, repeat affirmations that resonate harmoniously with her energy, such as 'I am worthy of love and respect,' or 'I fully embrace my inner strength and resilience.' Infuse these words with intention and deep belief, allowing their transformative power to permeate your being. This sacred practice not only enhances your personal empowerment but also contributes to healing the collective wounds that women have carried throughout history, transcending generations and fostering unity among us. By consciously acknowledging and embracing these divine qualities, we reclaim the narrative of femininity, honoring our unique individual journeys while simultaneously celebrating our shared experiences as women throughout the ages. In this sacred space, we strengthen our bond not only to one another but also to the divine feminine that has always resided within us, nurturing the connections that unite us in spirit and purpose. This journey becomes a powerful reminder of the immense strength we possess together and the enduring legacy we continue to build, shaping a brighter future for generations to come.

In addition to the profound benefits of individual meditation, engaging in group practices can significantly amplify the transformative power of the sacred feminine. By gathering with like-minded women who share similar values, aspirations, and intentions, we create a vibrant space for exchanging stories and personal experiences. This exchange not only fosters a nurturing and safe environment but also encourages vulnerability and authentic connections among participants, building trust and camaraderie. We can engage in guided meditations that delve deeply into profound themes such as healing, empowerment, and creativity, allowing for a more extensive exploration of these essential aspects of life. As a collective, we can invoke the energy of various goddesses, inviting their wisdom and guidance to flow through the group, thereby enriching the overall experience for everyone involved. This shared journey reinforces our understanding that we are not alone in our struggles and triumphs. It cultivates a deep sense of community and unwavering support among women, reminding us of the strength found in unity. Together, we can uplift, inspire, and empower one another, forging a powerful bond that transcends individual experiences while celebrating our collective strength and resilience. By coming together, we nurture an atmosphere of love and solidarity that enhances our growth and enriches our spiritual journeys. This communal aspect not only strengthens our individual paths but also deepens our connection to the sacred feminine energy that resides within us all.

As we navigate the intricate complexities and myriad challenges of modern life, embodying the sacred feminine emerges as an essential and vital aspect of our overall well-being and personal fulfillment. It is crucial to wholeheartedly embrace the rituals and meditations that resonate deeply with your unique and individual journey, allowing these practices to weave into the fabric of your daily existence. We must recognize that the sacred feminine is not merely an abstract concept but a living, breathing force that exists within each and every one of us, waiting to be acknowledged, nurtured, and expressed. By honoring our bodies, nurturing our spirits, and celebrating our unique and diverse paths, we do more than just contribute to a larger movement; we become active participants in a transformative process of healing and empowerment that transcends individual experience, connecting us to the greater whole of humanity. Through these meaningful practices, we can actively express the sacred feminine in a contemporary context, thereby inspiring future generations of women to rise, reclaim their power, and wholeheartedly embrace their divine essence with confidence and grace. This collective journey not only fosters community and connection but also allows us to honor our shared experiences and wisdom. In doing so, we create a supportive environment where everyone can thrive in their authentic selves. By engaging in this sacred exploration together, we can deepen our understanding of ourselves and each other, paving the way for a more compassionate, inclusive, and harmonious world for all. Embracing the sacred feminine is not just an individual endeavor; it is a unifying force that empowers us to uplift one another, creating ripples of positive change that extend far beyond ourselves.

Creating Sacred Spaces with Altars and Ceremonies

Creating sacred spaces is an essential and transformative practice for women who seek to honor and embody the sacred feminine in their lives. Altars and ceremonies serve as powerful and dynamic tools for connecting with divine energies, expressing heartfelt gratitude, and manifesting clear intentions. By intentionally and thoughtfully crafting these spaces, women can draw upon the rich and diverse tapestry of goddess archetypes and their unique attributes, inviting the profound wisdom of ancient traditions into modern contexts. This creative and meaningful act not only reflects personal beliefs and values but also fosters a deeper and more enriching connection with the feminine divine, a connection that resonates across various cultures and spans the breadth of time. Through these practices, women can cultivate a sacred environment that nurtures their spiritual journeys and honors the collective wisdom of the feminine. By engaging in this sacred artistry, women can also create a sanctuary that provides solace and inspiration, encouraging self-discovery and personal growth. Each altar becomes a unique expression of individual spirituality, shaped by personal experiences and aspirations. This intentional crafting of sacred spaces allows women to celebrate their journeys, acknowledge their struggles, and embrace their strengths. As they gather in these hallowed spots for reflection, meditation, or community rituals, they deepen their connection not only to themselves but to the collective feminine spirit that transcends generations. This practice empowers women to reclaim their sacred heritage and share it in a contemporary context, weaving together the ancient and the modern in a beautiful tapestry of honor and reverence.

An altar can be as simple or as elaborate as one desires, serving as a profound and tangible manifestation of our inner spiritual landscapes and aspirations. It serves as a powerful conduit for personal expression, allowing individuals to connect with the divine in a deeply meaningful way. An altar can hold representations of various goddess figures that inspire, empower, and uplift us, such as the nurturing energy of Demeter, the fierce independence of Artemis, or the transformative wisdom of Kali. Each item placed upon the altar can symbolize different aspects of the sacred feminine and invite specific energies into our lives, enriching our spiritual experience and deepening our connection to the divine in ways that resonate with our personal journeys.

The selection of items for the altar is not just a routine task; it is a deeply personal and intentional process that encapsulates individual stories and spiritual aspirations. This meaningful selection can include a diverse array of elements, such as crystals celebrated for their healing properties, vibrant flowers that evoke joy and positivity, images that inspire courage and resilience, and cherished items that hold unique significance and meaning for each person. Each piece chosen becomes a reflection of our unique narratives and experiences, serving as a constant reminder of our personal growth and spiritual evolution. By thoughtfully creating a sacred space that resonates with one's unique journey and spiritual path, women can cultivate an environment that is profoundly conducive to reflection, meditation, and personal growth.

This sacred space not only functions as a sanctuary for quiet contemplation but also transforms into a wellspring of inspiration and empowerment that can positively influence their daily lives. Such a sanctuary enables individuals to reconnect with their true selves, channeling the energies of the goddesses and divine forces. It allows for the embracing of the myriad aspects of the divine feminine that reside within us all, facilitating a deeper exploration of self and fostering a profound connection to the universe and its mysteries. By engaging in this sacred practice, individuals can discover solace, strength, and clarity, enriching their spiritual journeys and enhancing their overall well-being. This holistic approach to spiritual growth encourages a deeper understanding of oneself and the world, promoting a sense of belonging and empowerment that resonates throughout all aspects of life.

Ceremonies, whether experienced in quiet solitude or joyously shared with others in a vibrant communal setting, significantly amplify the profound and transformative experience of honoring the sacred feminine. These rituals can be thoughtfully crafted around the natural cycles of the earth, such as the ever-changing seasons, the phases of the moon, or significant life events, creating a harmonious rhythm that beautifully aligns with the essence of the divine feminine. Each ceremony serves as a valuable opportunity to express deep and authentic emotions, set meaningful intentions that resonate with our true selves, and release what no longer serves our higher purpose or spiritual growth. By engaging in these practices, we deepen our connection to ourselves and the universe, fostering a sense of belonging and spiritual awakening that enriches our lives and those around us. Simple yet profoundly impactful practices, such as lighting candles, chanting, drumming, or invoking the names of revered goddesses, can infuse these gatherings with a palpable sense of sacredness, connection, and deep reverence.

Through these shared and cherished experiences, women can cultivate a truly robust sense of community, mutual support, and empowerment that resonates beyond the moment. This reinforces the powerful idea that the sacred feminine flourishes most vibrantly in collective spaces where love, understanding, and compassion abound, encouraging each participant to embrace her own unique journey while simultaneously recognizing the profound interconnectedness of all women. It is within these nurturing environments that individuals can explore their inner selves, foster lasting friendships, and uplift one another in a spirit of solidarity. By fostering an environment rich in nurturing energy and collective wisdom, these ceremonies not only honor the sacred feminine but also inspire personal growth and collective healing. They invite participants to delve deeper into their spiritual practices, explore their emotions, and connect authentically with one another. As each woman shares her story and journey, the collective energy becomes a powerful force for transformation, reminding everyone of the strength and resilience found in unity. Gatherings create a sacred space where the divine feminine can thrive, fostering an ongoing legacy of empowerment and interconnectedness among women everywhere.

In exploring the rich tapestry of feminine spirituality practices, it becomes paramount to weave in a diverse array of healing and empowerment elements that resonate deeply with the multifaceted experiences of women across various cultures and backgrounds. Altars, in particular, can serve as powerful and transformative focal points for healing rituals, creating sacred spaces where women come together to honor their bodies, share their unique stories, and reflect on the transformative journeys that shape their identities. Incorporating healing herbs, crystals, and essential oils can significantly enhance the energy of the altar, turning it into a nurturing sanctuary that fosters both personal and collective healing.

By engaging in these profound and intentional practices, women can not only reclaim their unique narratives but also wholeheartedly embrace their bodies in all their diverse and beautiful forms. This enriching and transformative journey allows them to cultivate a deep and lasting sense of self-love and acceptance that transcends the ordinary boundaries of daily life and societal expectations. This sacred work not only facilitates the acknowledgment of the wounds of the past but also creates a vital and nurturing space to celebrate the immense resilience, courage, and strength inherent in the feminine spirit. Through these meaningful connections, we forge deep and lasting bonds that support both individual growth and communal empowerment, creating a vibrant mosaic of shared experiences that uplift, inspire, and transform all who participate in this deeply enriching journey of self-discovery and collective healing.

In this way, we not only honor the complexities of our past but also pave the way for a brighter, more inclusive future for everyone involved, fostering a collective spirit of unity and understanding that encourages further exploration and celebration of our unique identities. This journey is not merely about healing; it is fundamentally about thriving together as a community, building bridges of support, and nurturing a legacy of empowerment that will resonate through generations to come. By weaving our individual stories into the fabric of our shared existence, we create an environment where every voice is valued, and every experience contributes to the collective wisdom. Together, we embark on a path of discovery that not only highlights our differences but also celebrates the common threads that bind us, enriching our lives and the lives of future generations in ways that are profound and lasting. Through this commitment to each other, we illuminate the power of community, creating spaces for dialogue, growth, and joy that transcend the individual journey and resonate with the heart of humanity itself.

By coming together in this way, we not only honor our individual journeys but also contribute to a collective narrative that celebrates the richness of feminine spirituality. This leads to a more profound understanding of ourselves, each other, and the world around us. In doing so, we foster a sense of belonging and interconnectedness that empowers women to thrive together, reminding us that our shared experiences and collective wisdom are invaluable treasures that can guide us toward a more enlightened and harmonious existence.

Creating sacred spaces through altars and ceremonies serves as a profound invitation for women to fully embody the principles of the sacred feminine in their everyday lives. This practice encourages a transformative relationship with these ideals, inviting deeper introspection and connection. It not only fosters a more nuanced understanding of the rich and intricate mythology surrounding goddesses but also illustrates how these timeless narratives can meaningfully inform our modern experiences and perspectives. By consciously recognizing, honoring, and expressing the sacred feminine, women can cultivate a powerful sense of agency and empowerment, enriching their connection to their bodies, health, and overall well-being in ways that resonate deeply within. As we thoughtfully honor these cherished traditions and rituals, we celebrate not only our individual journeys of growth and transformation but also contribute to a collective rise of feminine power, wisdom, and strength in the world today. This shared commitment to honoring the sacred feminine fosters a supportive environment where all women can thrive. It encourages the development of a vibrant community that uplifts and inspires one another in the pursuit of holistic well-being, self-actualization, and the realization of our highest potential. Together, we can harness this energy to create a ripple effect that expands beyond ourselves, impacting the world around us in meaningful and transformative ways.

The Role of Nature in Feminine Spirituality

The intricate and complex bond between nature and feminine spirituality is profoundly intertwined with the very essence of womanhood, creating a rich and dynamic relationship that has evolved over centuries and continues to resonate deeply in contemporary society. For countless generations, women have sought solace and inspiration from the natural world, drawing on its innate wisdom, profound mysteries, and remarkable healing properties that have stood the test of time. Nature embodies the vital cycles of life—birth, growth, decay, and eventual rebirth—reflecting the myriad experiences and challenges that women navigate throughout their unique journeys, both individually and collectively. This deep and meaningful connection not only encourages women to embrace their inherent power fully but also empowers them to tap into the profound wisdom that emerges from living in harmony with the rhythms of the earth and its seasons. By recognizing and honoring these cycles, women gain a clearer understanding of their own unique paths and transformations, leading to greater self-awareness, empowerment, and a deeper appreciation of their roles within the greater tapestry of life and the universe.

Here we will plunge our hands deep into the fertile soil that is the myriad ways in which nature serves as a vital and enriching element of feminine spirituality, revealing its multifaceted contributions to personal growth, healing, and self-discovery. We will explore the insights offered by various goddess archetypes that embody different aspects of nature, the diverse array of spiritual practices that draw upon the power of the natural world, effective healing methodologies that integrate natural elements, and the holistic embodiment of the sacred feminine across cultures and traditions. We will examine how these elements intricately interweave with the natural world, creating a vibrant tapestry that fosters a comprehensive, fulfilling, and transformative spiritual experience for women everywhere. This exploration encourages women to reconnect with their roots, the wisdom that nature imparts, and the profound interconnections that bind them to the earth and each other. Through this journey, we aim to illuminate the pathways through which feminine spirituality and nature coalesce, enriching the lives of women and affirming their place within the cycles of existence that resonate so deeply throughout history and into the present.

Goddess archetypes across various cultures frequently draw their strength and unique attributes from the natural elements around us, serving as powerful symbols that resonate deeply with the multifaceted feminine experience. The Earth Mother, for instance, symbolizes not only fertility and nurturing but also the profound and enduring connection to the land, embodying the essence of creation and sustenance that has been revered through generations. This archetype reflects the cycle of life, with its intricate dance of birth, growth, decay, and renewal, serving as a reminder of the resilience and strength inherent in all women. Meanwhile, the Moon Goddess represents intuition, mystery, and the natural rhythms of life, highlighting the cycles and phases of the feminine journey that many women navigate, from adolescence to motherhood and beyond. Each goddess reflects a distinct and vital aspect of nature, such as the fierce protector or the wise elder, and in turn, encourages women to connect deeply with these archetypes within themselves, fostering a sense of identity and belonging. By recognizing, honoring, and embodying these divine figures, women can tap into their own inner power and wisdom, celebrating the sacred feminine that dwells in all of us. Engaging with these archetypes can provide a rich and nuanced framework for personal exploration and self-discovery, empowering women to find, embrace, and express their unique interpretation of femininity in the modern world. This engagement not only enhances individual growth but also fosters a profound sense of community, shared strength, and solidarity among women everywhere, encouraging them to uplift one another on their individual journeys. In doing so, women can create a tapestry of experiences that honors their collective heritage while paving the way for future generations, ensuring that the sacred feminine continues to thrive in a rapidly changing world.

Feminine spirituality practices are profoundly enriched by the natural world, offering an extensive and diverse array of rituals and meditations that not only honor but also celebrate the sacred feminine in its many beautiful and multifaceted forms. Nature serves as a breathtaking and awe-inspiring backdrop for these transformative practices, inviting women to fully immerse themselves in the elements—earth, water, air, and fire—in ways that resonate deeply with their inner selves.

Whether through a grounding meditation in a tranquil, lush forest filled with the sounds of chirping birds and the gentle rustling of leaves, or a cleansing water ritual performed by the expansive and rhythmic ocean waves that ebb and flow with the heartbeat of the Earth, these experiences profoundly enhance the connection to the feminine divine. Picture a vibrant fire ceremony held under the vast, starry sky that twinkles with endless possibility and wonder, where the flames dance with the same energy that fuels our spirits.

These immersive encounters significantly deepen the bond with the sacred feminine, cultivating a profound sense of peace and clarity while fostering a deeper awareness of the intricate interconnectedness of all life around us. They remind us that every being is part of a larger and beautifully complex tapestry of existence, woven together by unseen threads of love and intention.

In this way, the sacred feminine emerges not just as an abstract concept but as a living, breathing force that we can actively engage with, celebrate, and honor in our everyday lives, enriching our spiritual journeys and grounding us in the beauty of the world around us.

In this way, nature emerges as an incredibly powerful ally and a wise guide in the profound journey of spiritual growth. It encourages women to delve deeply into their inner landscapes while nurturing a harmonious relationship with the vibrant world around them. Through these sacred and transformative interactions with nature, women can tap into the nurturing energies of the earth, forging lasting bonds with their communities and wholeheartedly embracing the ancient wisdom intricately woven into the fabric of the natural world. This vital connection not only enhances personal growth but also invites a much deeper understanding of our unique place within the vast universe. It allows for transformative experiences that resonate on multiple levels, enriching the soul in profoundly meaningful ways.

By engaging thoughtfully with the ever-changing rhythms of nature, women cultivate a greater appreciation for the intricate cycles of life, drawing strength and inspiration from the earth's cycles of renewal and rest. This profound relationship fosters ongoing reflection and gratitude, leading to a more integrated and holistic approach to spirituality that honors both the nurturing feminine spirit and the environment that supports and sustains it. The sacredness of the natural world becomes a wellspring of inspiration, prompting women to embrace their innate power and creativity while recognizing the essential importance of stewardship of the earth. As they engage deeply with the natural world, they embark on a transformative journey that enriches their personal lives and contributes significantly to the collective healing of our planet. Through this deepened and meaningful connection with nature, women are empowered to become catalysts for positive change. They foster a profound sense of responsibility toward the environment and inspire others to honor the sacred feminine within themselves and the world that surrounds them. This journey not only enhances individual growth but also reinforces the interconnectedness of all beings, creating a ripple effect that nurtures both personal and collective well-being in the broader tapestry of life.

Healing and empowerment are not merely fundamental aspects; they are vital cornerstones of feminine spirituality, intricately woven into the rich and multifaceted tapestry of women's lives. Nature plays an essential and transformative role in these profound processes, acting not only as a sanctuary but also as a powerful source of strength, renewal, and inspiration. The earth generously offers a vast abundance of resources that are crucial for healing—herbs, crystals, and natural remedies that have been cherished, utilized, and revered by women for generations. These practices and beliefs are often lovingly passed down through the wisdom of our ancestors and the enduring traditions they cultivated over time, creating a legacy of knowledge that empowers women today. Engaging in a variety of practices such as herbalism, moon rituals, or simply spending time in the nurturing embrace of the great outdoors can yield profound and lasting effects on physical, emotional, and spiritual well-being. These activities create a harmonious balance that many seek in today's fast-paced and often overwhelming world. Furthermore, nature encourages women to fully embrace their bodies, cultivating a deep sense of body positivity, self-love, and acceptance that transcends societal expectations and limitations imposed by the world around them. By reconnecting with the natural rhythms of the earth, women not only heal from the burdens imposed by societal pressures but also reclaim their inherent power. This reclamation fosters a collective healing that resonates deeply throughout their communities, allowing them to become beacons of hope and resilience in a world that often challenges their strength. This shared experience inspires and empowers other women to embark on their own transformative journeys of self-discovery and empowerment, providing invaluable support and encouragement along the way. In doing so, they create a ripple effect that strengthens the bonds of sisterhood, nurtures the spirit of resilience in all women, and fosters a supportive network that uplifts and inspires future generations. This interconnectedness ensures that the truths of feminine spirituality continue to flourish, allowing women to celebrate their shared experiences and wisdom while paving the way for the empowerment of those who will come after them.

Mythology serves as a rich and intricate tapestry that beautifully embodies the enduring principles of the sacred feminine. It often illustrates the profound and intricate bond between women and the natural world, weaving together narratives that resonate through time and across diverse cultures. Legends from a wide array of traditions depict powerful goddesses who personify the earth, showcasing their nurturing qualities while also highlighting their fierce independence and remarkable resilience in the face of adversity. These timeless stories not only inspire women to view themselves as integral parts of a much larger narrative but also emphasize the critical importance of protecting our natural environment and preserving its beauty in a world that often takes it for granted. As contemporary women navigate the complexities and challenges of their lives, these ancient myths can serve as guiding lights, constantly reminding them of their inherent strength, boundless wisdom, and essential responsibility to honor, cherish, and protect the earth. This stewardship is vital not only for their own well-being but also for the well-being of future generations and the continuity of life itself. By connecting deeply with these narratives, women can find empowerment and inspiration that fosters a deeper understanding of their role in the sacred cycle of life and nature. Furthermore, these stories encourage women to embrace their connection to the earth, recognizing that their actions can create ripples of positive change. In a time when environmental issues are more pressing than ever, the wisdom of these ancient tales can fuel a collective movement toward sustainability and respect for the planet. Through the lens of mythology, women can reclaim their voices, celebrate their heritage, and actively participate in the preservation of the world around them, ensuring that the sacred feminine continues to thrive for generations to come.

In this world where we live, women are increasingly discovering and expressing the sacred feminine through a multitude of aspects within their everyday lives, transforming their unique experiences into powerful and transformative manifestations of spirituality. They are often actively integrating the profound wisdom of nature into their spiritual practices, which significantly deepens and enriches their connection to the world around them. From the principles of eco-feminism to holistic health and wellness, the tenets of feminine spirituality are beautifully intertwining with various contemporary movements. These movements empower women to reclaim, redefine, and elevate their connection to the earth and to one another in profoundly meaningful ways that resonate deeply within their souls. This journey is not merely about personal empowerment; it is fundamentally about fostering a vibrant, nurturing, and supportive community of women who uplift and inspire one another in embracing their divine nature and inherent strengths. By recognizing and honoring the crucial role of nature in feminine spirituality, women can draw upon its abundant wisdom, healing properties, and resilience. This allows them to celebrate the sacred feminine in every conceivable aspect of their lives, enriching their personal journeys while simultaneously enhancing their collective experiences. As they weave together a rich tapestry of shared growth, understanding, and mutual support, women create a powerful network that nurtures their spiritual evolution. This connection fosters a deeper sense of belonging and interconnectedness among all who participate in this transformative journey. Together, they cultivate an environment where each woman's voice is heard, valued, and celebrated, reinforcing their collective commitment to embracing the sacred feminine and its profound impact on their lives and communities.

Healing and Empowerment

The Power of Feminine Healing Modalities

The exploration of feminine healing modalities presents an incredibly profound and enriching gateway into the sacred feminine, a vast and dynamic realm that is brimming with wisdom, empowerment, and transformative potential. These modalities, often deeply rooted in ancient traditions and holistic practices, serve not only as vital pathways for personal healing but also as powerful tools for collective transformation among women. By fully embracing and engaging with these diverse healing practices, women can reconnect with their innate power, nurture their overall well-being, and cultivate a deeper understanding of their bodies, minds, and spirits.

This enriching journey invites us to honor the goddess archetypes that reside within each of us, recognizing that each archetype embodies unique attributes and qualities that can profoundly guide our individual and collective healing journeys. Through this exploration, we can empower ourselves and each other, creating a vibrant and supportive community where healing is not only celebrated but also shared and amplified. This fosters deeper connections and understanding among women of all backgrounds and experiences.

In this sacred space, we can learn from one another, uplift our spirits, and collectively embrace the transformative power of feminine healing practices. This shared journey not only enhances our personal growth but also strengthens the bonds of sisterhood, allowing us to navigate life's challenges together and celebrate our victories. By cultivating an environment where every woman feels valued, heard, and empowered, we create a sanctuary of love, support, and understanding that can profoundly impact our lives and the lives of those around us. Together, we can embody the essence of healing and empowerment, leading to a brighter future for ourselves and our communities.

In numerous cultures across the globe, goddess figures stand as profound symbols representing various dimensions of feminine energy, embodying a rich tapestry of qualities such as strength, compassion, intuition, creativity, and resilience. By actively invoking and connecting with these potent archetypes, women can tap into an extensive reservoir of healing energy that resonates intimately with their own unique life experiences and personal journeys. For instance, establishing a meaningful connection with the nurturing essence of Mother Earth through the goddess Gaia can inspire women to embrace holistic self-care practices. This connection cultivates a profound sense of grounding, stability, and balance in their lives amid the chaos and unpredictability of modern existence. Similarly, channeling the fierce and unyielding warrior energy of the goddess Durga can empower women to confront challenges head-on, enabling them to stand resiliently in the face of adversity. They can draw strength from her unwavering spirit, fierce determination, and relentless courage, reminding them of their own capacity for resilience.

These archetypes invite us to fully embody their attributes, serving as a powerful reminder that we are never truly alone in our struggles. Support often exists in various forms, frequently appearing in unexpected ways. They highlight the enduring truth that the wisdom of the ancients can resonate deeply within our contemporary lives, guiding us through our journeys and encouraging us to embrace our own inner power, creativity, and authenticity as we navigate the complexities of existence. By recognizing and honoring these divine figures, we not only foster a deeper connection to our own feminine essence but also unlock the transformative potential that lies within each of us. This journey encourages a celebration of our individuality and collective strength, reinforcing the idea that the path we walk is enriched by the legacies of those who came before us. Through this recognition, we can cultivate a more profound understanding of ourselves and the world around us.

Feminine spirituality practices play an essential and transformative role in harnessing the profound energy inherent in a wide array of healing modalities. By engaging in rituals and meditations that honor and celebrate the sacred feminine, individuals not only create transformative sacred spaces but also empower women to delve deeply into their inner landscapes and emotional depths with heightened intensity and awareness. Simple yet profoundly meaningful practices, such as lighting a candle to symbolize intention or crafting a vision board that vividly reflects personal aspirations and dreams, can serve as powerful acts of manifestation and healing that resonate on multiple levels—both personally and collectively. These rituals cultivate a profound sense of connection to the divine feminine while also nurturing a deeper, more compassionate relationship with oneself and with others.

As women immerse themselves in these enriching practices, they frequently discover newfound clarity, inner peace, and a renewed sense of purpose, direction, and fulfillment in their lives. This transformative journey not only leads to a more balanced and harmonious existence but also empowers them to navigate life's challenges and joys with an enhanced sense of empowerment, grace, and authenticity. Through this exploration, women can connect with their true selves and foster a community of support and understanding, creating an environment in which they can thrive. By sharing their experiences and insights, they establish a network of solidarity that reinforces the importance of these practices, encouraging others to embark on their own journeys of self-discovery and empowerment. The collective energy generated through these shared experiences amplifies the healing potential of feminine spirituality, inspiring a broader movement toward collective well-being and personal transformation.

The sacred feminine offers an incredibly profound and transformative lens through which we can deeply explore essential aspects of women's health, fertility, and body image. By understanding the body not merely as a physical entity but as a sacred vessel imbued with profound purpose and significance, women are empowered to reclaim their personal narratives and actively challenge the often rigid and restrictive societal expectations that distort and undermine body image. Various healing modalities, including womb healing, menstrual cycle awareness, and somatic practices, serve as powerful and effective tools that enable women to embrace and honor their bodies' natural rhythms and cycles in a deeply meaningful and fulfilling way.

By fully and deeply honoring the sacred feminine that resides within our bodies, we cultivate a nurturing and supportive space for self-acceptance and unconditional love. This process fosters a much healthier, more positive, and enriching relationship with ourselves and our identities. Such transformative journeys not only enhance our individual well-being but also encourage a collective shift towards a more compassionate and holistic understanding of women's experiences and challenges. This reclamation of the sacred feminine transcends mere self-love; it is a radical and revolutionary act of empowerment that invites women to celebrate their bodies as sacred entities, inherently worthy of reverence, dignity, and respect.

Engaging in this journey allows women to fully embrace their individuality, inner strength, and unique beauty, thereby reinforcing the importance of honoring and valuing the diverse experiences of womanhood in all its forms. By fostering this vital connection to the sacred feminine, women can create a supportive and inclusive community where shared experiences and collective wisdom flourish. This leads to significant healing and transformation for everyone involved. In this way, the journey becomes not just a personal endeavor but a shared movement that uplifts and celebrates all women. It encourages a deeper understanding of what it truly means to be a woman in today's complex and often challenging world, where the need for connection, solidarity, and support is more crucial than ever before. Together, we can build a future that honors the sacred feminine and nurtures the well-being of all women, paving the way for a more compassionate society.

As contemporary women navigate the intricate complexities of modern life, the embodiment of the sacred feminine becomes not just vital but essential to our well-being and personal growth. By consciously and thoughtfully integrating these powerful healing modalities into our daily practices, we not only honor and celebrate our own unique journeys but also uplift, empower, and inspire the vibrant communities surrounding us. The true power of feminine healing modalities lies not only in the profound personal transformations they facilitate but also in the collective awakening they inspire within us all, creating a ripple effect that resonates far beyond our individual selves.

When women come together, sharing their rich and varied stories, diverse experiences, and unique perspectives, they weave a powerful tapestry of healing that transcends generations and fosters an enduring sense of unity. In this sacred sisterhood, we discover not just strength and resilience but also a shared commitment to rise together in celebration of the divine feminine that resides within each of us. This collective journey illuminates our paths, fosters deeper connections, and encourages us to support one another in a world that often seeks to divide. It reminds us of the profound power we hold when we unite in love and purpose, demonstrating that our combined energies can create transformative change not only within ourselves but also in the wider world. Together, we can nurture a future that embodies the essence of the sacred feminine, enriching our lives and the lives of those around us.

Collective Healing through Sisterhood and Community

Collective healing is an incredibly transformative journey that flourishes within the nurturing and supportive bonds of sisterhood and community. This journey resonates with the timeless wisdom of the sacred feminine, a wisdom that has echoed across diverse cultures and throughout the ages, leaving a profound impact on human history. In our fast-paced modern lives, where feelings of disconnection and isolation often prevail, the need for nurturing and supportive relationships among women becomes not just important but absolutely paramount for our overall well-being and emotional health.

This sisterhood acts as a safe sanctuary, a sacred space where we can openly share our vulnerabilities, celebrate our unique individual strengths, and empower one another to rise in our true authenticity and inherent power. By uniting in our shared experiences and collective stories, we create a powerful and intricate tapestry of healing that honors and uplifts the divine feminine within each of us. This enriching process fosters growth, resilience, and a deeper sense of connection in our interconnected lives, reminding us that we are never alone in our struggles.

As we engage in this sacred journey, we not only heal ourselves but also contribute significantly to the healing of those around us. This creates a ripple effect that extends far beyond our immediate circles, touching many lives and bettering our communities. By fostering a collective spirit of empowerment and solidarity, we transcend boundaries and limitations, creating a rich environment where every voice is heard and valued.

This journey revitalizes our spirits and strengthens the very essence of sisterhood, encouraging us to embrace our shared humanity and the beauty inherent in our individual journeys. Together, we weave a legacy of strength, compassion, and understanding that resonates through generations, paving the way for future generations to experience the profound interconnectedness that arises from genuine support, love, and understanding. In this way, we nurture a vibrant community where everyone can thrive, fostering not only individual growth but also collective flourishing that impacts the world around us.

Throughout the course of history, a diverse and rich array of goddess archetypes has beautifully epitomized the essence of community and the profound power inherent in collective healing. Figures such as Demeter, the nurturing Earth Mother, and Brigid, the revered Celtic goddess of creativity and healing, serve as vital reminders of our innate capacity to support and uplift one another through shared rituals and communal practices. These powerful archetypes not only inspire us but also challenge us to cultivate and nurture environments in which we can openly express our feelings, seek constructive guidance, and foster resilience in times of need.

By drawing on their rich and varied attributes, we engage in collective endeavors that not only promote deep healing but also significantly strengthen our bonds—whether through group meditations that deepen our connections, healing circles that nurture our spirits, or even simple gatherings that provide a welcoming and inclusive space for us to share our personal stories and experiences. Together, we create a vibrant and intricate tapestry of healing that transcends individual struggles and celebrates our shared journey, reminding us that we are never truly alone in our experiences, and that together we can navigate the complexities of life with compassion and understanding.

Feminine spirituality practices play an essential and transformative role in nurturing a deep communal bond among us, creating a sacred space where we can experience profound connection and understanding. By engaging in rituals that honor our sacred selves and the unique essence each of us brings to the collective, we not only foster personal growth but also encourage a richer, more meaningful connection with one another. This deepening of relationships enhances our understanding of ourselves and each other in remarkably profound ways.

For instance, creating a shared altar or participating in seasonal celebrations invites us to immerse ourselves in the cycles of nature and the inherent rhythms of our bodies. Such practices instill a sense of reverence and appreciation for the world around us, allowing us to experience the divine in every moment and reminding us vividly of our place within the vast universe. These practices serve as powerful reminders that we are all integral parts of a larger whole, beautifully echoing the ancient wisdom of the Earth and the nurturing spirit of the goddess, which has guided women throughout history.

As we honor and celebrate our individual journeys, we simultaneously weave a supportive web that uplifts, empowers, and nourishes each woman in the community. This creates a rich tapestry of shared experiences, mutual respect, and genuine connection that reinforces our unity. Such interconnectedness fosters a profound sense of belonging and collective strength, reminding us that together, we can navigate the complexities of life with grace, resilience, and unwavering support for one another.

In this way, we cultivate a vibrant community that not only celebrates individuality but also cherishes and honors the beautiful bonds that unite us all. This collective spirit reminds us of the immense power we hold when we stand together, reinforcing the idea that our shared experiences can illuminate the path for others and enrich the lives of everyone involved. Furthermore, as we engage in these practices, we deepen our commitment to one another, understanding that our collective energy elevates not just our individual spirits but the very essence of our community, fostering an environment where creativity, compassion, and love can flourish abundantly.

The myths and legends of the sacred feminine offer

profoundly rich lessons on healing, empowerment, and the transformative journey of self-discovery that resonate powerfully across generations and cultures. These narratives illuminate the incredible resilience of women who have faced tremendous adversity, emerging not only stronger but also more determined individuals, often buoyed by the unwavering support, love, and solidarity of their sisters in spirit and action. The stories of powerful goddesses—such as Kali, who embodies transformation, liberation, and fierce independence, and Athena, who symbolizes wisdom, strategic thinking, and courageous intellect—provide us with compelling archetypal narratives that deeply resonate with our own struggles, challenges, and eventual triumphs.

By diving into these timeless tales together, we cultivate a profound sense of belonging, connection, and purpose that transcends individual experiences and unites us in a shared understanding of our collective journey. This collective exploration fosters an environment where we can recognize and embrace the goddess within ourselves, guiding us as we navigate the intricate complexities and myriad challenges of modern life. In doing so, we honor the legacies of these powerful figures, empowering ourselves to rise above our challenges with grace, resilience, and unwavering strength. This empowerment, in turn, inspires others along the way to discover and embrace their own inner strength and potential.

Through this transformative journey, we create a ripple effect of empowerment that extends far beyond ourselves, touching the lives of those around us and igniting a shared passion for growth and self-discovery within our communities. By sharing these stories and experiences, we not only strengthen our bonds with one another but also contribute to a larger movement that celebrates the divine feminine. This movement encourages every individual to explore their unique path and embrace the boundless power within. Together, we can foster a nurturing environment where our collective wisdom gives rise to new possibilities, enriching our lives and the lives of those with whom we share this journey.

In embracing the sacred feminine, we not only honor our past but also pave the way for future generations to thrive, ensuring that the legacy of strength, resilience, and empowerment continues to flourish in an ever-evolving world.

In today's rapidly evolving world, embracing the sacred feminine is not just important; it is absolutely crucial for our collective healing, transformation, and renewal. As women, we find ourselves on a profound journey that encourages us to deeply appreciate our bodies, acknowledge our complex and often conflicting emotions, and joyfully celebrate our diverse, vibrant, and multifaceted expressions of femininity. By cultivating a culture of steadfast support, genuine understanding, and deep acceptance, we empower one another to break free from the limiting chains of societal expectations and nurture our true, authentic selves. Through this shared journey of exploration, growth, and rediscovery, we create inclusive spaces where we can heal, thrive, and uplift one another in meaningful, impactful ways.

We recognize the sacred feminine not merely as an

abstract idea, but as a vibrant, living force that unites us in sisterhood and community. This recognition serves as a powerful reminder of our shared strength and resilience, illuminating the deep interconnectedness that binds us together as one. It fosters a profound sense of belonging and purpose that enriches our lives, reminding us that we are not alone in our struggles and triumphs. As we embrace and embody the sacred feminine, we invite a wave of transformative energy that resonates throughout our communities, inspiring future generations to honor their own journeys and the unique expressions of femininity that arise. In this way, we not only affirm our individual identities but also weave a rich tapestry of connection that celebrates the beauty of womanhood in all its forms.

Techniques for Personal Empowerment

A variety of methods for achieving personal empowerment are absolutely crucial for women who aspire to fully embrace their inner goddess and adeptly navigate the often complex and multifaceted challenges of modern life. Throughout the transformative journey of self-discovery and personal empowerment, recognizing and honoring the sacred feminine within can serve as a profoundly transformative experience that nurtures growth, healing, and profound self-awareness. By engaging with a variety of enriching practices that honor and celebrate the essence of feminine spirituality, women can cultivate not only immense strength and resilience but also a deeper understanding of their unique paths, identities, and potential. This journey encourages women to connect with their intuition, fostering a sense of belonging and purpose in a world that often undermines their inherent power and worth.

This section dives into a range of techniques that resonate deeply with the essence of the sacred feminine, inviting women to reclaim their personal power, wholeheartedly celebrate their individuality, and express their authentic selves more fully and confidently in all areas of their lives. Through this comprehensive exploration, readers will find not only inspiration but also practical tools and resources to support and enhance their empowerment journey. These resources will encourage them to step into their true essence and potential, helping to illuminate the path toward a life imbued with authenticity, joy, and purpose. These techniques will empower women to embrace their unique voices, foster community connections, and break free from societal constraints that may limit their growth. By integrating these practices into daily life, women can create a sanctuary of strength and self-expression, ultimately leading to a more liberated and fulfilling existence. This process is not merely about personal growth; it is a call to action for women everywhere to unite in their shared experiences, uplift one another, and collectively forge a future where the sacred feminine is celebrated and revered in all its forms.

One of the most profound and transformative techniques for personal empowerment is the deeply enriching and meaningful practice of ritual. Rituals serve as an incredibly powerful means of connecting with the divine feminine, offering individuals a unique and valuable opportunity to engage with their spirituality in a way that resonates profoundly with their own beliefs and personal preferences. Whether it's lighting candles in a sacred space to invoke tranquility and peace, performing a moon ritual to honor the beautiful cycles of nature and its transformative energy, or creating a personal altar adorned with meaningful symbols of strength, femininity, and resilience, rituals provide a tangible and impactful way to express intentions, desires, and aspirations.

Engaging in these sacred acts not only fosters a profound sense of personal connection but also cultivates a vibrant sense of community and belonging among like-minded individuals. This collective practice allows women to align their energies harmoniously with those of their ancestors and goddess archetypes, creating a powerful sacred circle that nurtures empowerment, growth, and collective strength. Such a practice reinforces a shared commitment to spiritual development and personal evolution, allowing for deeper exploration and understanding of one's own path. By participating in rituals, individuals can find a renewed sense of purpose and a clearer vision of their aspirations, strengthening their resolve to navigate life's challenges with grace and confidence.

Meditation is an essential and transformative technique that plays a crucial role in unlocking the personal power of women. Through the dedicated practice of meditation, women can cultivate a much deeper and more meaningful connection to their inner selves, allowing them to access the profound wisdom and intuition that often remain dormant amid the chaotic rush and relentless demands of daily life. Engaging in guided meditations specifically focused on the sacred feminine can significantly empower women to visualize their inherent strengths, confront and overcome their deepest fears, and fully embrace their unique gifts and abilities. These meditative practices serve as a catalyst for self-discovery, enabling women to tap into their inner reservoirs of strength and resilience.

Furthermore, incorporating practices such as mindfulness and breathwork not only enriches this experience but also enables women to ground themselves in the present moment while elevating their spirits to new heights of awareness and understanding. The combination of these techniques encourages a holistic approach to personal growth, fostering both mental clarity and emotional balance. By committing dedicated time and effort to the practice of meditation, women can foster a greater sense of self-awareness, gain clarity in their thoughts and emotions, and cultivate a profound sense of inner peace and tranquility.

All of these elements work in harmony to contribute to a much more empowered, fulfilling, and enriched existence. This empowered state allows women to navigate life with confidence and grace, supporting them in overcoming obstacles and achieving their aspirations. As they delve deeper into their practice, they find themselves not only transforming their own lives but also inspiring others in their journeys toward self-empowerment and self-love.

Incorporating the energy of goddess archetypes into daily life serves not only as a powerful technique for personal empowerment but also as a profoundly transformative journey of self-discovery that can significantly impact women's lives in countless ways. Women are presented with an extraordinary opportunity to delve deep into the multifaceted qualities represented by various goddesses. These include the nurturing aspect embodied by Demeter, the fierce independence and strength exemplified by Artemis, or the profound wisdom that Athena offers to those who earnestly seek it. By thoughtfully reflecting on how these attributes resonate within them, women can uncover deeper insights into their own identities, desires, and life paths, paving the way for a more authentic existence.

Participating in practices like journaling about these experiences can reveal valuable insights and affirmations that not only ignite inspiration but also nurture significant personal growth and resilience. By consciously embodying the traits of these divine figures, women can fully step into their power, embracing their unique potential to create meaningful and lasting change in their lives and the broader world around them. This journey enriches their life experiences and fosters a strong sense of community, while also strengthening connections with others who share similar aspirations and challenges.

The process leads to a more profound understanding of themselves, their innate strengths, and their place in the intricate tapestry of life. It encourages the formation of a supportive network that celebrates each woman's unique journey as they navigate their paths together, sharing wisdom and experiences that uplift and inspire one another. Through this collective journey, women can foster an environment where each individual's narrative is valued, creating a rich tapestry of shared experiences that not only enhances personal growth but also amplifies the collective power of women in society.

Addressing the sacred feminine in relation to the body is not just important; it is absolutely crucial for fostering a profound sense of personal empowerment and growth across multiple interconnected levels of existence. Understanding the deep and intricate connection between the sacred feminine and essential aspects of women's health—including fertility, body image, and emotional well-being—allows for a holistic and comprehensive approach to overall wellness that simply cannot be overlooked or underestimated in today's fast-paced world. By wholeheartedly embracing transformative practices such as yoga, expressive dance, mindfulness, and nurturing self-care rituals, women can cultivate a deeply loving and supportive relationship with their bodies that transcends the physical realm, reaching into the emotional and spiritual dimensions of their existence.

Celebrating the various cycles of life—such as menstruation, motherhood, and all the significant transitions in between—as sacred experiences powerfully underscores the vital importance of fostering a sense of reverence for the female form and its remarkable capabilities. This celebration serves as a poignant reminder of the incredible wisdom inherent in these experiences, highlighting the unique narratives each woman carries within her.

By honoring their bodies and recognizing the profound wisdom they possess, women can effectively reclaim their power, embrace their unique and individual journeys, and wholeheartedly celebrate the extraordinary beauty of the sacred feminine that resides within each of them. This transformative journey not only enriches their lives but also empowers them to inspire others along the way, creating a ripple effect of empowerment and awareness that resonates throughout their communities and beyond. Through this collective awakening, women can further amplify their voices and contributions, fostering a supportive environment that elevates the entire sisterhood and encourages a shared understanding of the sacred feminine's profound impact on both personal and communal well-being.

As they engage with these practices and insights, women can build a stronger foundation of self-acceptance and love, contributing to a brighter, more enlightened future for themselves and those around them. This journey cultivates a space where the sacred feminine is not just acknowledged but celebrated in all its forms and manifestations, enriching individual lives while enhancing the collective experience of womanhood. This allows for a deeper connection among women and a renewed appreciation for the cycles that define their existence, fostering an environment where each woman feels empowered to share her story and wisdom, thereby weaving a rich tapestry of shared experiences that honors the sacred feminine in every aspect of life.

Through these powerful and transformative techniques—ritual, meditation, goddess embodiment, and body awareness—women can embark on an extraordinarily life-changing journey that guides them toward profound personal empowerment and deeper self-discovery. Embracing the sacred feminine not only opens the door to the exploration of individual strengths but also illuminates the shared experiences that cultivate a rich and meaningful collective sense of empowerment within diverse communities. As women begin to recognize, honor, and joyfully celebrate their inherent power through these enriching practices, they not only honor the divine feminine within themselves but also in their connections with others, creating a sense of unity that enhances their shared journey.

This awakening generates a ripple effect of healing and strength that transcends individual lives and resonates across generations, nurturing a lasting legacy of empowerment that is lovingly passed down through time. In celebrating the sacred feminine, women not only uplift themselves but also play a crucial role in contributing to a broader awakening of the collective feminine spirit, inspiring others along their unique paths. This movement encourages the creation of a compassionate world that deeply honors, cherishes, and respects the divine in all its multifaceted forms, leading to a more harmonious, balanced, and fulfilling existence for everyone involved.

By taking part in these transformative practices, women forge strong bonds that reinforce community ties, instilling a profound sense of unity and shared purpose that enriches the journey for all. This collective effort fosters a supportive environment where every woman can truly thrive, encouraging each individual to express their authentic self. Together, they create a vibrant tapestry of empowerment that weaves through the very fabric of society, inspiring future generations to embrace their own journeys of self-discovery and personal empowerment. In doing so, they lay the groundwork for a brighter, more inclusive future where every voice is valued, and every journey is celebrated.

Embracing Vulnerability as Strength

Embracing vulnerability as a source of strength is a profoundly transformative journey that resonates deeply with the concept of the sacred feminine. Throughout various cultures and mythologies, goddess archetypes beautifully encapsulate this principle, serving as powerful reminders that vulnerability is not merely a sign of weakness but rather an essential facet of our shared humanity that deserves both recognition and respect. Take, for instance, the nurturing qualities of Demeter, who, in her profound grief over the loss of her beloved daughter, brings forth the cycles of life and death, illustrating that even in our deepest sorrow, there exists remarkable potential for renewal and rebirth, highlighting a testament to the resilience of the human spirit. Similarly, the fierce compassion of Kali exemplifies how embracing chaos and destruction can lead to the creation of new beginnings and transformative opportunities, emphasizing that vulnerability can serve as a potent catalyst for profound healing, personal growth, and empowerment.

By honoring and exploring these rich goddess archetypes, we learn to accept and embrace our own vulnerabilities as vital pathways to inner strength and resilience. This exploration not only facilitates a deeper understanding of ourselves but also reveals our intricate interconnectedness with the world around us. Such a journey enriches our personal experiences, fostering a greater sense of community and shared humanity among us. It allows us to connect with others on a more profound level, forging bonds that transcend superficial barriers and cultivate an environment of empathy, compassion, and mutual support. Collective understanding strengthens our ability to navigate life's myriad challenges, reinforcing the powerful idea that together, we can rise from our vulnerabilities to create a more compassionate and resilient world.

In this way, we embrace a shared journey toward healing that unites us in our quest for understanding and connection, nurturing a landscape where our collective experiences of vulnerability become the foundation for a more empathetic and harmonious existence. By recognizing and celebrating these aspects of ourselves and each other, we create a rich tapestry of human experience, one that honors the beauty found in our shared struggles and triumphs. Through this lens, we can transform our vulnerabilities into a source of empowerment, inspiring not just personal growth but also a broader movement toward unity and compassion in our communities.

In our modern lives, embracing vulnerability invites us to engage deeply in a rich tapestry of various feminine spirituality practices that profoundly celebrate and honor our authentic selves. These rituals, which center around self-reflection—such as journaling, meditation, and creative expression—serve as invaluable tools that significantly aid us in acknowledging our fears and insecurities. These practices help us delve into a deeper understanding of ourselves, revealing layers of complexity and insight. By creating a sacred space for our emotions, we can explore them freely, without any judgment or fear of dismissal. This nurturing and safe environment enables us to investigate the profound depths of our souls, much like the inspiring goddess figures we admire and look up to in our spiritual journeys.

As we courageously bring our vulnerabilities into the light, we reclaim our personal power, establishing a more profound connection to the divine feminine that resides within us all. This connection fosters an enriching sense of community and shared experience among women of all ages, backgrounds, and walks of life. The collective journey we embark upon not only strengthens our bonds but also empowers us to uplift one another as we navigate our individual and shared paths. It serves as a powerful reminder that together, we can flourish, support each other, and thrive in our quests for growth, empowerment, and self-discovery. Through these shared experiences, we begin to realize the true strength of our interconnectedness, encouraging us to embrace our unique journeys while standing united in our pursuit of authenticity and transformation. Each step we take together not only deepens our personal journeys but also enriches the collective spirit, reminding us of the beauty and strength we gain from our connections with one another.

Healing through vulnerability not only encourages us to recognize the profound interconnectedness of our experiences as women, but also highlights the unique beauty of each individual journey. When we courageously share our stories and struggles, we create a vibrant tapestry of collective healing that honors and celebrates every woman's path. This shared vulnerability can serve as an immensely powerful tool for empowerment, allowing us to learn from one another and uplift each other, especially in our darkest moments. Just as the goddess Artemis fiercely protects and champions her fellow women, we too can embody this spirit by offering unwavering support and deep compassion to those around us. Together, we can transform our pain into strength, weaving a rich narrative of resilience that not only celebrates but also honors the sacred feminine in all its forms.

In doing so, we foster a community where every voice is heard and valued, paving the way for deeper connections and understanding. The act of sharing our vulnerabilities not only strengthens our bonds but also illuminates the diverse paths we walk, each filled with its own challenges and triumphs. This journey of mutual support can inspire us to rise above adversity, reminding us of the incredible power that lies within our shared experiences. As we embrace this journey together, we cultivate an environment where healing flourishes, and the sacred feminine shines brightly through the unity we create.

The myths and legends that embody the principles of the sacred feminine often depict a profound strength found within vulnerability, illustrating the deep and intricate connection between our inner fears and our remarkable capacity for growth and transformation. For instance, the compelling and transformative tale of Inanna's descent into the underworld serves as a powerful illustration of her extraordinary willingness to confront her deepest fears and insecurities head-on, shedding light on the vital importance of facing the unknown. Through this harrowing journey, Inanna emerges from the experience not only more empowered but also profoundly enlightened, showcasing the incredible resilience that can arise from facing one's darkest moments.

Similarly, our own personal journeys may require us to bravely confront the shadows that linger within us, embracing those facets of ourselves that we often choose to hide away or ignore, sometimes even from our own conscious awareness. This introspective process can indeed be daunting and challenging; however, it is precisely within these moments of raw honesty and deep self-reflection that we can uncover and truly discover our most authentic selves, unlocking the potential for profound personal growth and transformation. By drawing inspiration from these ancient and timeless stories, we can empower ourselves to face our vulnerabilities with unwavering courage and resilience.

We come to understand that these vulnerabilities are not only integral to our individual growth but also essential to our ongoing transformation and evolution as human beings. Through this journey of self-discovery and acceptance, we come to realize that embracing our vulnerabilities is a crucial step toward a fuller, richer, and more meaningful existence. This embrace allows us to connect deeply with ourselves and fosters connections with others in a world that often encourages disconnection and isolation. In doing so, we pave the way for a more compassionate and understanding society, one where collective healing and personal empowerment can flourish. By recognizing that our struggles are shared and our vulnerabilities are universal, we can cultivate a profound sense of community and empathy, enriching our experiences and promoting a deeper understanding of the human condition.

In today's world, women are increasingly embodying and expressing the sacred feminine in profound and diverse ways that honor their vulnerabilities as strengths. Whether through activism, artistic and creative expression, or fostering nurturing relationships, contemporary women are courageously redefining what it truly means to be powerful and resilient. By wholeheartedly embracing our vulnerabilities, we actively challenge societal norms that dictate that strength must be devoid of emotion or sensitivity. This transformative shift not only empowers us as individuals but also creates a powerful ripple effect, inspiring others around us to reclaim their own vulnerabilities and recognize their inherent worth.

As we celebrate the sacred feminine, we warmly invite all women to understand that by embracing our vulnerability, we are not only honoring ourselves but also contributing to a larger movement of healing, connection, and empowerment within our communities. Together, we can forge a path toward a more compassionate and inclusive future. By acknowledging and celebrating our vulnerabilities, we can create spaces where emotional authenticity is valued, and where every woman feels seen and heard. This journey is not just about individual growth; it is about collective strength and solidarity. As we stand together, we can uplift one another and inspire a new generation to live boldly, embracing both their strengths and their vulnerabilities as essential components of their identities.

Sacred Feminine in Mythology

Myths from Around the World

Myths from around the world serve as profound narratives that not only entertain but also illuminate the essence of the sacred feminine. Each culture has intricately woven its own vibrant tapestry of stories, rich with divine female figures who embody strength, wisdom, and nurturing qualities. From the Indigenous tales of the Earth Mother, who nurtures all life with her boundless compassion and unwavering support, to the captivating Greek legends of Athena, the goddess of wisdom and warfare, and Artemis, the fierce protector of wildlife and women, these myths reflect the myriad ways in which women have been revered, celebrated, and honored throughout history in diverse and meaningful contexts.

For adult women embarking on the exploration of their spiritual paths, these timeless stories offer a powerful reminder of the inherent divinity within themselves, as well as the vast potential for empowerment that lies in recognizing and embracing these profound ancestral connections. By delving into these ancient narratives, women can uncover deeper layers of their identity, drawing inspiration from the rich legacy of feminine power that has persisted through the ages, reminding them of the strength and resilience of their heritage. This engagement not only encourages them to honor their own journeys and the sacred feminine within but also fosters a deep sense of belonging to a lineage of powerful women who have shaped the world in countless significant and transformative ways across cultures and eras.

One of the most compelling aspects of these myths is their remarkable ability to resonate across vast stretches of both time and geography, creating connections that span generations and cultures. The goddess figures often embody a variety of archetypes that profoundly speak to the complex and multifaceted nature of womanhood. This allows women from diverse backgrounds to find common ground in their experiences and shared struggles, fostering a sense of unity and understanding. For instance, the Hindu goddess Kali, with her fierce and transformative energy, stands as a powerful testament to the dual forces of destruction and rebirth. She illustrates how endings can lead to new beginnings, symbolizing the cyclical nature of life that many women navigate throughout their journeys. Kali's presence serves as a reminder of the resilience inherent in womanhood, highlighting the strength that arises from overcoming adversity.

In contrast, the nurturing aspect of Demeter, the Greek goddess of the harvest, emphasizes the essential importance of fertility and sustenance. This highlights the critical role women play in nurturing life and providing for their families in both physical and emotional ways, often serving as the backbone of their communities. Demeter's story reinforces the idea that nurturing extends beyond mere survival; it encompasses the emotional and spiritual support that women offer, creating a foundation for growth and stability within families and societies.

By engaging with these diverse and richly layered archetypes, women can reflect on their own unique life experiences and challenges, finding both solace and inspiration in the timeless stories that resonate with and echo their personal journeys. Through this deep connection with these powerful figures, they can gain profound insights into their identities, the myriad roles they play in the world, and the immense power they hold in shaping their own destinies. This fosters a sense of empowerment and unity among women across different cultures and times, reinforcing the idea that their struggles and triumphs are part of a broader narrative that transcends individual experiences. In this way, the myths not only celebrate the diverse experiences of women but also encourage them to embrace their unique paths while recognizing the shared strength in their collective stories.

Rituals and practices inspired by these powerful myths can serve as profound pathways to connect deeply with the sacred feminine. For instance, creating altars that honor specific goddesses can provide a dedicated and focused space for meditation, contemplation, and thoughtful reflection, allowing women to immerse themselves fully in this enriching spiritual journey. Women can incorporate a diverse array of elements associated with these deities—such as vibrant flowers, healing crystals, meaningful symbols, and even personal tokens—into their rituals. This effectively links their own unique experiences with the divine feminine energy that these timeless myths embody. Such practices not only deepen one's spiritual connection but also play a significant role in facilitating healing, growth, and empowerment on multiple levels.

Through this transformative process, women can reclaim their unique narratives and embrace their identities with renewed confidence, transforming their lives through the enlightening lens of the sacred feminine. Engaging in these rituals fosters a strong sense of community and support among women, further enhancing the experience of shared spirituality, collective empowerment, and connection to one another. By coming together in this meaningful and intentional way, women can create a nurturing environment that amplifies their individual journeys, strengthens their bonds as a collective force, and cultivates a deeper understanding of their shared experiences.

This unity not only enriches their spiritual lives but also encourages a greater exploration of their inner selves, fostering resilience and a sense of belonging that uplifts and inspires all involved. This shared experience creates a transformative impact on their lives and the communities they are part of, reinforcing the importance of collective rituals in nurturing a deeper connection to the sacred feminine and to one another. Through these shared practices, women can inspire one another, celebrate their unique paths, and embark on a journey of self-discovery that resonates far beyond their individual experiences.

The relevance of these myths extends deeply into modern contexts, where women continue to embody the principles of the sacred feminine in their everyday lives and experiences. Contemporary artists, writers, and activists draw profound inspiration from these ancient stories, utilizing them as a strong foundation to challenge prevailing societal norms and promote healing within their communities. By recognizing and celebrating the sacred feminine in their creative work, these women honor the rich legacy of the goddesses who came before them, forging a meaningful bridge between the past and the present. This intricate intertwining of mythology and modern expression not only fosters a sense of community among women but also encourages collective empowerment and the sharing of sacred stories that resonate across generations.

By doing so, they ensure that the essence of these myths remains vibrantly alive and relevant in today's world, inspiring future generations to connect deeply with their heritage and embrace the power that lies within themselves. This ongoing dialogue between the ancient and the contemporary not only enriches artistic expression, but also reinforces the importance of storytelling as a means of cultural preservation. As these women continue to explore and reinterpret these timeless narratives, they cultivate a deeper understanding of the divine feminine, inviting others to join in this transformative journey. In this way, the sacred feminine becomes a powerful catalyst for change, igniting a movement that celebrates the strength, wisdom, and resilience of women throughout history and into the future.

Understanding the myths surrounding the sacred feminine enables women to embrace their own bodies and experiences with a deeper sense of compassion, heightened awareness, and profound respect for their unique journeys. Many of these narratives intricately weave together themes of health, fertility, and body image, inviting women to engage in meaningful, introspective reflection on their relationships with themselves and the world around them. By reclaiming and redefining the narratives that revolve around feminine divinity, women can cultivate a profound sense of belonging, empowerment, and acceptance within their own bodies, fostering a nurturing environment that encourages self-love, personal growth, and holistic well-being.

This journey through these rich and complex myths not only honors the sacred feminine but also empowers each woman to rise and thrive, embodying her own unique expression of the divine in a way that is authentic, true, and deeply resonant with her individual spirit. In this transformative process, the myths evolve from mere stories of the past into vibrant, living transformations that resonate in the present. They encourage women to embrace their journeys fully, celebrate their inherent strength, wisdom, and resilience, and to find solidarity with one another in shared experiences. This exploration becomes a powerful catalyst for change, allowing women to connect more deeply with themselves and their communities, fostering a sense of unity and empowerment that transcends individual narratives.

Lessons from the Goddesses: What They Teach Us

Throughout the vast and intricate tapestry of history, goddesses have emerged as powerful and enduring symbols of the sacred feminine, each one embodying a unique and diverse set of attributes and lessons that resonate profoundly with women from a wide array of cultures and across countless generations. From the nurturing qualities of Demeter, who beautifully represents the essence of motherhood, fertility, and abundance, to the fierce and unapologetic independence of Kali, a formidable warrior who stands boldly against darkness and oppression, these divine figures serve as vivid and compelling reminders of the multifaceted nature of womanhood and the extensive spectrum of experiences it encompasses.

By discovering the rich and varied stories that surround these goddesses, along with the distinct characteristics that define their personas, we can glean profound insights and invaluable wisdom that significantly aid us in navigating our own lives more effectively, empowering us to embrace both our strengths and our vulnerabilities alike. The narratives woven around these powerful and inspiring goddesses not only serve as a wellspring of inspiration and encouragement but also invite us to celebrate our individuality while acknowledging and honoring our collective experiences as women.

These stories prompt us to reflect thoughtfully on both our unique and shared journeys, fostering a deeper and more meaningful connection to the sacred feminine that resides within each and every one of us. This connection encourages us to honor the invaluable wisdom that has been passed down through generations, enriching our understanding of ourselves and each other. In doing so, we not only empower ourselves but also uplift and enrich the lives of those around us, creating a vibrant tapestry of shared understanding and unwavering support that uplifts and strengthens all women.

This collective spirit of unity and purpose enhances our journey, fostering an environment where every woman can thrive and feel valued. As we navigate the complexities of our modern lives, these goddesses remind us of the strength found in community and the importance of nurturing our spiritual and emotional well-being. By embracing the lessons they impart, we cultivate resilience and compassion, ensuring that we not only support our own growth but also the growth of those who walk alongside us. In this interconnected journey, we discover the power of solidarity, enabling us to face challenges with courage and grace, while celebrating the diverse experiences that shape our identities as women. Together, we weave a legacy of empowerment that echoes across generations, fostering a world where every woman's voice is heard and honored.

The lessons imparted by the goddesses extend far beyond mere mythology; they hold significant relevance to our modern existence, resonating deeply with our daily lives and struggles in profound ways that can profoundly transform our understanding of ourselves and the world around us. For instance, the resilience embodied by Persephone imparts powerful lessons about transformation and rebirth, serving as a poignant reminder that even in our darkest and most challenging times, we possess the incredible power to emerge anew and stronger, much like the seasons change and renew with each cycle. This cyclical nature of life is a crucial aspect of feminine spirituality, inviting us to engage in rituals and practices that honor both our light and shadow, thus embracing the wholeness of our being. By consciously incorporating these timeless lessons into our lives, we cultivate a deeper understanding of ourselves and our unique journeys, fostering a sense of empowerment that can lead to meaningful change on a personal level and within our broader communities. Embracing these teachings can inspire us to create a more compassionate, connected, and harmonious world, where we acknowledge the interconnectedness of all beings and the importance of nurturing our inner strength in ways that promote healing, resilience, and growth within ourselves and those around us. These goddesses serve as guiding figures, encouraging us to navigate life's complexities with grace, wisdom, and courage, enriching our experiences and fostering a community rooted in empathy, support, and collective growth. Their enduring messages challenge us to be more mindful and intentional in our actions, reminding us that we are all part of a larger tapestry of existence, intricately woven together through our shared experiences, desires, and aspirations. By embracing these insights, we empower not only ourselves but also those in our communities, creating a ripple effect of positive change that can transcend generations, encouraging a legacy of compassion and understanding that resonates far beyond our immediate surroundings.

The sacred feminine encourages us to fully embrace

our bodies and recognize the profound wisdom they inherently possess. Goddesses such as Venus and Lakshmi not only celebrate beauty and abundance but also invite us to thoughtfully and courageously redefine our notions of body image and self-worth in a much deeper and more expansive context. By actively engaging in practices that honor our physical selves—whether through purposeful movement, deep meditation, or nurturing rituals—we can connect on a much deeper and more meaningful level with the sacred feminine that resides within us. This profound connection not only enhances our self-esteem but also promotes holistic well-being, empowering us to reclaim our bodies as sacred vessels of power, creativity, and divine expression. In doing so, we create a harmonious and nurturing relationship with ourselves, fostering a deep sense of empowerment and joy that resonates throughout all aspects of our lives, enriching our experiences and relationships along the way.

By embracing this transformative journey, we unlock the immense potential for personal transformation and healing, allowing the sacred feminine to guide us toward a more profound understanding of our own worth and the beauty that lies within. This journey is not merely personal; it extends to our interactions with others, inspiring them to embark on their own paths of self-discovery and empowerment. This collective journey contributes to a broader awakening and appreciation of the sacred feminine energy that exists in all of us, creating a ripple effect that enhances not only our individual lives but also the lives of those around us. As we come together in this shared experience, we foster a community rooted in love, acceptance, and the celebration of our unique and divine expressions of the feminine.

In delving into the rich treasury of myths and legends that envelop these formidable goddesses, we uncover an array of powerful narratives that not only challenge but also subvert the societal norms and expectations historically imposed upon women. The stories of goddesses such as Artemis and Freyja serve as compelling illustrations of the vital importance of autonomy, self-determination, and personal empowerment in a world that often seeks to diminish these essential qualities. These myths inspire us to boldly forge our own unique paths, encouraging us to rise above the constraints society frequently imposes, which seek to confine and limit our potential. By wholeheartedly embracing the profound lessons imparted by these powerful figures, we can cultivate a deep and abiding sense of agency in our lives. This empowerment can serve as a catalyst, motivating and encouraging others to embark on their own journeys of self-discovery and personal growth.

Such collective empowerment not only enriches our individual experiences but also fosters a vibrant community characterized by support and understanding. In this nurturing space, women uplift one another in their quests for fulfillment and authenticity, creating an environment ripe for shared growth, resilience, and solidarity. Together, we can build a dynamic network that celebrates our diverse journeys, sharing our stories and insights while championing the strength found in unity. By standing together in this way, we not only acknowledge our individual struggles and triumphs but also weave a stronger fabric of solidarity that benefits us all, reinforcing the importance of collaboration and mutual support in our collective pursuits for empowerment and fulfillment.

The teachings of the goddesses serve as a profound reminder of the deep sacredness that resides within our experiences as women. They invite us to honor our unique and diverse narratives while simultaneously recognizing the shared threads of connection that weave us all together in a beautiful tapestry of existence. As we thoughtfully integrate the profound lessons imparted by the goddesses into our daily lives, we not only celebrate the sacred feminine but also empower ourselves and one another to rise in strength, grace, and authenticity.

In embracing this transformative journey, we not only honor but also perpetuate the rich legacy of these divine figures, embodying their timeless wisdom and nurturing the transformative power of the sacred feminine in our contemporary world. This journey invites us to deepen our understanding of ourselves, encouraging a journey of self-discovery that inspires us to fully embrace our true essence. It fosters a vibrant community where we uplift each other, harnessing our collective energy to shine brightly together. By recognizing the importance of these teachings, we cultivate a space of mutual support and understanding that empowers us to navigate the complexities of modern life with confidence and resilience. Together, we can create a world where the sacred feminine is celebrated and integrated into every aspect of our lives.

The Role of Myth in Modern Feminine Spirituality

In the intricate tapestry of modern feminine spirituality, myths serve as powerful vessels that carry the profound wisdom of our ancestors and illuminate the diverse paths we tread today. These narratives, often deeply steeped in the rich experiences of women throughout history, provide both a mirror and a map, reflecting the struggles, triumphs, and sacred qualities that are inherently woven into the feminine experience. By delving into goddess archetypes from various cultures across the globe, we can uncover connections that resonate deeply with mythological figures embodying attributes such as strength, compassion, creativity, and resilience. These figures serve as vital reminders that we are part of a much larger narrative—one that transcends time and space, inviting us to honor and embrace the divine feminine within ourselves and to recognize its profound significance in our lives and communities.

Through this exploration of myth, we not only celebrate our rich heritage but also empower ourselves to manifest these essential qualities in our daily existence. Engaging with these myths allows us to foster a stronger sense of identity and purpose, helping us navigate our journeys while cultivating a deeper understanding of the interconnectedness of all women throughout history. This journey of exploration also encourages us to form bonds with one another, creating a supportive network that nurtures our growth and understanding. In doing so, we can inspire future generations to continue this legacy of honoring the divine feminine, ensuring that its wisdom endures and flourishes in an ever-evolving world, transforming the way we perceive ourselves and our roles within it. By embracing these timeless narratives, we can weave a brighter future, rooted in the strength of our shared past.

Mythology invites us to reimagine our own stories through the transformative lens of the sacred feminine, urging us to delve into deeper layers of meaning, connection, and understanding. Through rituals and practices that honor these powerful mythical figures, women can tap into an extraordinary and profound wellspring of empowerment, healing, and self-discovery that transcends the boundaries of time and culture. Whether it's invoking the nurturing energy of Demeter, the fierce transformative strength of Kali, or the profound wisdom of Athena, these archetypes offer invaluable guidance and unwavering support, assisting us as we navigate the intricate complexities and challenges of modern life.

Engaging deeply with these rich and multifaceted myths allows women to reclaim their narratives, transforming personal struggles into powerful sources of strength, resilience, and inspiration that resonate on a universal level. In this way, the sacred feminine emerges not merely as an abstract concept but as a vibrant lived reality that empowers us to fully embrace our unique journeys. It inspires us to honor our authentic selves while fostering a deep sense of community with others who share similar paths and experiences. This connection encourages a collective awakening, reminding us that we are never alone in our journeys but are part of a larger tapestry woven from shared stories and experiences, reinforcing the idea that we are all interconnected.

By exploring these myths, we not only find strength within ourselves but also cultivate a profound sense of belonging, solidarity, and mutual support. This enrichment of our lives becomes even more significant as we walk together on this shared journey toward understanding and empowerment, transforming our individual paths into a collective quest for deeper insight and connectedness. In doing so, we embrace the essence of the sacred feminine, allowing it to guide us through the complexities of life and illuminate the way toward a more empowered existence.

The healing potential of myth in feminine spirituality represents a profoundly significant aspect that merits our complete attention and appreciation. Myths frequently delve into enduring themes such as loss, renewal, and the cyclical nature of existence, resonating deeply with the rich and varied experiences women encounter as they navigate the complexities of change and transformation in their lives. By intentionally invoking and integrating these powerful narratives into our healing practices, we can cultivate a sacred and nurturing space that empowers us to fully embrace the intricate processes of grieving, celebrating, and evolving into our fullest selves.

Techniques such as guided meditations, engaging storytelling circles, and ritualistic practices centered around revered goddess figures can facilitate significant shifts in our perceptions of self-worth, body image, and personal empowerment. Engaging with these transformative myths not only supports our individual healing journeys but also fosters a profound sense of connection among us, contributing to the collective healing of our communities. This interconnectedness enhances the bonds we share with one another, enriching our overall spiritual journeys and enabling us to thrive together in a shared experience of growth, transformation, and mutual support.

By recognizing and honoring the wisdom embedded within these myths, we nurture our spirits and create a vibrant tapestry of shared experiences that enrich our lives and those of others around us. Embracing these narratives can truly help us navigate the myriad challenges we face, as we weave our own unique stories of resilience and empowerment into the intricate fabric of our collective existence. Such engagement not only uplifts our individual spirits but also reinforces the profound unity among us, allowing us to draw strength from one another as we journey forward together. In doing so, we honor the rich legacy of feminine spirituality and its enduring capacity to heal and inspire.

In today's world, the sacred feminine expresses itself in profoundly transformative and multifaceted ways through the myriad methods women employ to embody and intricately weave mythological stories into the very fabric of their everyday lives. As we confront societal pressures that frequently challenge our autonomy, self-acceptance, and overall well-being, the timeless wisdom of the goddesses offers a powerful counter-narrative that resonates deeply within us. This ancient wisdom not only urges us to celebrate our uniqueness but also to fully embrace and appreciate our bodies in all their diverse forms and complexities. Women are actively reclaiming their narratives and identities by engaging in transformative practices that honor their bodies and spirits. These practices, such as dance, yoga, and meaningful self-care rituals, nurture our inner selves and reinforce our vital connection to the sacred feminine. They also cultivate a profound sense of empowerment that is deeply rooted in both ancient wisdom and contemporary resilience.

By wholeheartedly embracing these practices, we create a sacred space for healing and growth, allowing ourselves to flourish in a world that continually seeks to define us and often overlooks our true potential. In doing so, we not only honor our individuality but also contribute to a collective movement that inspires others to recognize and reclaim their inherent power. This shared journey fosters a vibrant community of support, understanding, and solidarity among women everywhere, encouraging us to uplift one another and celebrate our collective strength. As we stand together in this transformative process, we deepen our connection to the sacred feminine, reminding ourselves and each other of the profound beauty and power that lies within us, waiting to be acknowledged and expressed.

The role of myth in modern feminine spirituality is not only essential but also profoundly transformative, serving as a vital bridge that intricately connects the rich narratives of the past with the vibrant realities of the present day. As we delve deeply into the intricate tapestry of goddess stories and their many attributes, we uncover not only a profound source of inspiration but also a powerful sense of belonging to a much larger lineage of women who have traversed similar journeys throughout history and across diverse cultures. By wholeheartedly embracing these timeless myths, we cultivate a deeper understanding of our unique experiences while simultaneously celebrating the sacred feminine that resides within ourselves and within each other. This process fosters a sense of unity and empowerment that transcends individual boundaries and nurtures our collective spirit.

In this joyous celebration of our shared heritage, we rise together, energized and empowered by the timeless stories that have shaped our identities and the divine feminine energy that continues to guide and uplift us on our individual paths. Each myth serves as a poignant reminder of our shared strength, resilience, and the profound interconnectedness of our journeys. This interconnectedness encourages us to honor the past while boldly forging our own paths forward into the future. In doing so, we not only enrich our spiritual lives but also contribute to a collective awakening that honors the wisdom of those who came before us. This awakening inspires future generations of women to embrace their own stories and identities, reminding them of the power that resides within. As we share these narratives with one another, we create a legacy of empowerment that uplifts not only ourselves but also those who will follow in our footsteps, ensuring that the sacred feminine continues to thrive and evolve.

Reclaiming Myths for Contemporary Empowerment

Reclamation of time-honored myths for contemporary empowerment is not merely an essential journey; it is a profound and transformative adventure for women who seek to forge a deep, meaningful connection with the sacred feminine both within themselves and in the world around them. As we immerse ourselves in the rich and intricate tapestry of goddess myths from a diverse array of cultures, we uncover narratives that resonate profoundly with our modern struggles, aspirations, and triumphs. These ancient stories are not just remnants of the past; they stand as powerful symbols and archetypes that offer us invaluable guidance, inspiration, and a profound sense of belonging in today's complex and often chaotic landscape. By actively engaging with these myths, we have the unique and empowering opportunity to reclaim a sense of power and agency that has often been overlooked or sidelined in the traditional narratives of history.

This enriching and transformative process allows us to weave our own unique stories of strength, resilience, and empowerment, enabling us to redefine our identities, embrace our authentic selves, and assert our rightful place in the world. In doing so, we not only honor and celebrate the wisdom of our ancestors but also pave the way for future generations of women to find their voices, assert their power, and continue the legacy of empowerment. Through this exploration, we can cultivate a deeper understanding of our shared experiences and acknowledge the diverse perspectives that have shaped the journey of women throughout history. By embracing these myths, we can foster a collective consciousness that supports and uplifts one another, creating a vibrant community of women who are empowered to take action, inspire change, and contribute to a more equitable and just society. This journey of reclaiming myths is not just about individual empowerment; it is about weaving a larger narrative that connects us all and fuels the ongoing movement for women's rights and liberation.

The goddess figures that populate these ancient myths embody an extraordinary and diverse range of attributes, spanning from the nurturing and life-giving aspects of Demeter, who represents fertility and the intricate cycles of nature, to the fierce independence and transformative power of Kali, who symbolizes strength, destruction, and rebirth. Each goddess serves as a representation of various facets of the feminine experience, encouraging us to explore and fully embrace the multiplicity of our identities and the complexities that come along with them. In doing so, we can find true empowerment through the acknowledgment of our inherent complexities and contradictions. Engaging deeply with these archetypes not only allows us to see ourselves reflected in their rich and varied stories but also offers a profound sense of validation and a meaningful pathway to personal growth and self-discovery. This exploration can ignite a spark that inspires us to reclaim our own narratives and unique experiences, urging us to step boldly into our own power, authenticity, and self-awareness.

These powerful goddesses remind us that embracing our inner strength and understanding our multifaceted nature are essential for effectively navigating the complexities of life. They encourage us to celebrate the different roles we play as we journey through our existence, as each role contributes to our overall understanding of ourselves and our place in the world. By recognizing and honoring these diverse aspects of femininity, we empower ourselves to confront challenges with resilience and grace, fostering a deeper connection to both ourselves and those around us.

Feminine spirituality practices provide a rich and transformative framework through which we can honor and actively celebrate the sacred feminine in our daily lives, enriching our existence with profound meaning. Engaging in a diverse array of rituals, meditations, and creative expressions that are deeply rooted in powerful and time-honored myths serves as essential tools for healing, empowerment, and profound personal growth. By thoughtfully incorporating these practices into our everyday routines, we create sacred spaces that not only allow us to connect with the divine essence within ourselves but also foster a sense of community and shared experience among those who participate in these transformative journeys.

Whether it's through a simple daily meditation invoking a particular goddess or a more elaborate ritual that celebrates the ever-changing cycles of the moon and the intricate rhythms of nature, these practices ground us firmly in the present moment while simultaneously linking us to the ancestral wisdom and enduring strength of the countless women who have come before us, shaping both history and spirituality. Embracing these cherished traditions not only enriches our spiritual journey but also deepens our understanding of the sacred feminine that resides within us all. It empowers us to express our unique voices in a world that often yearns for the nurturing energy and compassionate presence of the divine feminine, reminding us of the importance of nurturing ourselves and one another as we walk this path together.

As we navigate the intricate complexities and multifaceted challenges of modern life, the healing and empowerment offered by the sacred feminine emerge as increasingly vital and essential elements of our existence. The myths we explore are not simply stories; they serve as profound frameworks for understanding our personal and collective healing journeys, which are deeply intertwined with the rich tapestry of the human experience. By delving into the struggles and triumphs of various goddesses, we can find immense solace in the comforting knowledge that we are not alone in facing our challenges and adversities, which are often universal in nature and resonate across time and cultures. These powerful narratives encourage us to actively seek out community and support, reminding us that healing is frequently a shared and communal experience, intricately woven into the fabric of connection and solidarity with others.

By reclaiming the timeless wisdom embedded in these myths, we not only foster resilience and empowerment but also create a profound sense of unity, both individually and collectively. This lays the groundwork for a stronger and more unified foundation for our growth, transformation, and healing journey as we look toward the future with hope and intention. This journey not only enriches our lives but also deepens our understanding of the sacred feminine's role in guiding us through the complexities of existence. It illuminates pathways that may have once seemed obscured or out of reach, revealing new insights and perspectives. In embracing this wisdom, we cultivate a sense of belonging and purpose that empowers us, allowing us to face the future with courage and clarity, fully prepared to engage with the world and its myriad challenges. In doing so, we affirm our commitment to the ongoing process of healing and transformation.

The sacred feminine transcends the notion of a static concept; it embodies a dynamic, living, and breathing force that continuously evolves, adapts, and transforms with each generation that comes and goes. In contemporary contexts, women are not only embodying but also vibrantly expressing the sacred feminine in a remarkable and astonishing array of diverse, impactful, and powerful ways. From activism and leadership roles to self-care practices and movements advocating for body positivity, women are actively reclaiming their narratives, redefining what it truly means to be empowered in a world that often seeks to diminish their voices and contributions. By embracing the rich myths, stories, and traditions that celebrate the sacred feminine, we can inspire one another to rise, reclaim our stories, and honor the divine essence that resides within each and every one of us.

This journey of reclamation is not solely about honoring the past and acknowledging its deep significance; it is fundamentally about shaping a future where the sacred feminine is not only celebrated but also cherished and empowered in every facet of our lives. This empowerment allows us to cultivate a deeper connection to ourselves, each other, and the world around us, fostering a collective spirit that uplifts, nurtures, and enriches our communities in profound ways.

As we navigate this transformative path together, we pave the way for a more inclusive and harmonious existence that honors the sacred feminine in all its diverse forms. Each step we take invites us to deepen our understanding and appreciation of the sacred feminine's role in society, encouraging conversations that break down barriers and build bridges. This collective journey is about recognizing the strength in unity, celebrating our shared experiences, and elevating the voices of those who have been historically marginalized. In doing so, we not only honor the sacred feminine but also create a vibrant tapestry rich with the stories and contributions of women from all walks of life. Together, we can envision and enact a future where the sacred feminine is not merely acknowledged but revered, ensuring that it continues to illuminate our paths and inspire generations to come.

Sacred Feminine in Our Contemporary World

Women Leaders and the Sacred Feminine

In a world that has often celebrated and prioritized masculine ideals of leadership, the emergence of women leaders stands as a profound and transformative testament to the resurgence of the sacred feminine. These remarkable women, whether they are making significant strides in the realm of politics, thriving in the competitive landscape of business, or passionately engaging in the vital work of community organizing, embody qualities that have traditionally been associated with feminine archetypes—nurturance, intuition, collaboration, and compassion. By wholeheartedly embracing these attributes, they are not only fostering environments that encourage collective growth and healing but also actively challenging the entrenched status quo and redefining what it truly means to lead in today's society.

The concept of the sacred feminine goes far beyond mere theory; it is a dynamic and living energy that empowers women to confidently step into their roles as leaders. This empowerment occurs while they honor and celebrate their unique contributions to society, as well as the diverse perspectives they bring to the table in various arenas. As these women rise to prominence, they illuminate the path for future generations, demonstrating that leadership can be inclusive, compassionate, and transformative, reshaping the landscape for all.

The goddess archetypes from diverse cultures provide not only profound and transformative insights into the myriad qualities of the sacred feminine but also serve as a wellspring of inspiration that contemporary women can embody, celebrate, and honor with immense joy and deep reverence. Figures such as Kali, revered as the fierce and unwavering protector, embody unparalleled strength and resilience in the face of adversity; she serves as a powerful reminder of the inner warrior residing within every woman, urging them to tap into their latent power when confronted with life's myriad challenges. Through her fierce energy, women are encouraged to confront their fears and embrace the strength that lies within, empowering them to rise above obstacles and embrace their true selves.

Aphrodite, beautifully representing the essence of love, passion, and beauty, inspires women to wholeheartedly embrace their sensuality, creativity, and the vibrant energy that accompanies self-expression. She reminds them that their allure and charm are integral parts of their identity, deserving of celebration without hesitation or reservation. Her essence encourages women to revel in their individuality and to express themselves fully, recognizing that each woman's unique beauty contributes to the rich tapestry of life.

Meanwhile, Demeter, the nurturing and compassionate mother figure, resonates deeply within the hearts and spirits of women who are earnestly striving to reclaim their innate power and authenticity in a world that often seeks to undermine it. She encourages them to cultivate nourishment and support, not only for themselves but also for others in their communities. In doing so, she fosters a sense of connection, collaboration, and belonging, allowing women to uplift one another as they navigate the complexities of modern life.

Each archetype presents a unique and compelling facet of feminine strength, resilience, and empowerment, inviting women to explore their own identities, personal experiences, and emotional landscapes in a meaningful and reflective way that fosters profound personal growth and transformative self-discovery. By connecting with these ancient symbols and rich narratives, women can gain invaluable clarity on their individual paths, recognizing that their leadership styles, approaches, and personal journeys are as diverse and multifaceted as the goddesses themselves. Each archetype offers varied and rich lessons that can be applied to modern life, serving as guiding lights in times of uncertainty and confusion, illuminating paths that may have previously seemed obscured or challenging.

These archetypes, each in its own distinct and significant way, offer guidance, wisdom, and inspiration for the contemporary journey. They encourage women to embrace their unique gifts, acknowledge their strengths, and honor the sacred feminine that resides within. This process fosters a deeper connection to themselves and to one another, creating a supportive network of shared experiences and collective empowerment that enriches the lives of all women. It enables them to uplift and inspire each other as they navigate their unique journeys, leading to a more profound sense of solidarity, understanding, and mutual respect among them. In this shared journey, the sacred feminine flourishes, illuminating the path for future generations of women to follow.

Feminine spirituality practices play a vital and transformative role in honoring and manifesting the sacred feminine that resides within every woman. Through a diverse array of rituals, meditations, and various spiritual exercises, women are afforded the unique opportunity to deeply connect with their inner wisdom, intuitive insights, and the rich tapestry of their emotional landscape. These practices create a sacred space that fosters profound reflection, healing, and empowerment, enabling individuals to reconnect with their true essence and authentic selves.

Whether it's through the simple yet powerful act of lighting a candle, participating in a nurturing and supportive women's circle, or engaging in creative expressions such as art or writing, these rituals facilitate a deep and meaningful connection to their genuine selves. They help align women with the potent energies of the sacred feminine, which can be profoundly transformative. By engaging in these practices, women cultivate resilience, strength, and clarity—qualities that are essential for effective leadership and meaningful contributions in today's ever-evolving and dynamic world. This journey not only enriches their personal lives but also enhances their ability to inspire and uplift others, creating a ripple effect of positive change. These feminine spirituality practices not only serve as a pathway toward individual growth but also contribute to the collective empowerment of women everywhere, fostering a community where shared experiences deepen the bonds of sisterhood and mutual understanding. In this sacred space, women can explore their identities, celebrate their uniqueness, and embrace the power of their voices, further amplifying the impact of their contributions to the world around them.

The principles of the sacred feminine express themselves in profoundly transformative ways, manifesting through an exceptionally diverse and vibrant array of healing and empowerment techniques that resonate deeply with various communities around the globe. This interplay creates a rich tapestry of support and inspiration that is both dynamic and inclusive, reflecting the unique experiences of women and their allies. Women leaders frequently draw upon holistic approaches, which not only prioritize emotional and spiritual well-being but also seamlessly integrate traditional leadership methods with innovative practices that boldly challenge the status quo. This integrative and multifaceted perspective actively encourages leaders to cultivate and nurture environments that emphasize the critical importance of mental health, emotional intelligence, and robust community support. These essential elements are crucial for fostering sustainable growth and collective flourishing, providing a foundation for resilience in the face of adversity.

By actively addressing the collective wounds and challenges that women face in society, these visionary leaders not only empower themselves but also uplift their communities, fostering a deep sense of cohesion and solidarity as a unified whole. This dynamic and ongoing process creates a powerful ripple effect of healing and transformation that transcends individual experiences, nurturing a collective spirit that is vital for social change. It fosters a profound sense of unity, resilience, and interconnectedness among diverse groups, paving the way for lasting and meaningful change in the broader social landscape. Such change not only benefits countless generations to come but also inspires future leaders to carry forward this vital work with renewed passion and purpose. Through this unwavering commitment, they ensure that the principles of the sacred feminine continue to thrive and evolve, enriching our collective journey and enhancing our ability to face future challenges together.

As contemporary women navigate the intricate and often challenging complexities of modern life, they embody the sacred feminine in a multitude of diverse and vibrant ways. This embodiment manifests through their deeply personal journeys, ambitious professional endeavors, and unwavering resilience in the face of adversity. The rich myths and timeless legends that encapsulate the essence of the sacred feminine serve as powerful guiding lights, continually reminding women of their inherent strength and the profound importance of solidarity among one another. By celebrating their bodies, wholeheartedly embracing their health and well-being, and honoring their unique individual paths, women can redefine what it truly means to be a leader in today's world.

In this transformative journey, the sacred feminine emerges not only as a powerful source of inspiration but also as a compelling call to action that resonates across cultures and backgrounds. It invites women everywhere to rise, reclaim their power, and courageously share their unique gifts and talents with the world around them. In doing so, they foster a vibrant sense of community and empowerment, encouraging one another to break barriers and challenge societal norms. This collective effort not only uplifts individuals but also contributes to the creation of a brighter, more inclusive future for generations to come, where the voices of women are celebrated and their contributions recognized.

Art, Music, and the Expression of the Feminine

Art and music have long served as powerful and transformative mediums for the expression of the sacred feminine, allowing women to channel their unique experiences, deep emotions, and profound spiritual insights into tangible and meaningful forms of creativity. Across diverse cultures and historical epochs, the creative arts have consistently provided women with a voice—an essential platform for self-expression, a sacred space for introspection and reflection, and a vital means of connection to the divine and the cosmos. We delve into how these artistic expressions not only celebrate the essence of the feminine spirit but also serve as vital conduits for healing, empowerment, and collective transformation within communities. Through the enriching lens of art and music, we honor and recognize the myriad ways in which the sacred feminine manifests in our lives and the world around us, fostering a deeper appreciation for its profound impact on our spiritual journeys.

This exploration invites us to reflect on the interconnectedness of creativity and spirituality, revealing how the sacred feminine continues to inspire, uplift, and guide us, leading us toward a more profound understanding of ourselves and our place within the universe. As we engage with these artistic expressions, we uncover the layers of meaning and emotion that contribute to our collective consciousness, enriching not only our individual paths but also the shared experience of humanity as we navigate the complexities of existence together.

The journey into the realm of art and music allows us to tap into an ancient wisdom that resonates deeply within us, reminding us of the strength and resilience inherent in the feminine spirit. Each brushstroke, note, and rhythm becomes a testament to the struggles and triumphs of women throughout history, creating a rich tapestry of narratives that connect us across time and space. By celebrating these artistic expressions, we not only honor the past but also pave the way for future generations to explore their own voices within this vibrant lineage. Thus, 'Goddesses Rising' becomes not just an exploration, but a celebration of the enduring legacy of the sacred feminine, inviting us to participate in a transformative journey that nurtures our souls and enriches our communities.

The goddess archetypes embody a rich and intricate tapestry of diverse attributes and qualities that resonate profoundly with both our personal experiences and the broader collective narratives shaping our cultures and societies. Artists and musicians frequently draw inspiration from these timeless archetypes to convey their nuanced and deeply felt perspectives on femininity, skillfully weaving these potent symbols into their creative expressions. For example, the nurturing essence of the Earth Mother can be beautifully represented through the soothing and evocative melodies found in folk music, where her spirit nurtures feelings of comfort, warmth, and a profound sense of connection among listeners. This invites them to experience not just a feeling of belonging but also an emotional sanctuary that fosters healing, understanding, and a deep sense of peace in a chaotic world that often feels overwhelmingly turbulent.

In a similar vein, the fierce energy embodied by the Warrior Goddess may inspire dynamic and powerful anthems that strongly resonate with themes of strength, resilience, and empowerment. These remarkable works encourage individuals to confront life's challenges head-on, enabling them to rise above adversity with unyielding confidence and determination, embracing their inner strength as they navigate and grapple with difficult circumstances. By exploring the rich narratives and vibrant symbols associated with these divine figures, we uncover profound layers of meaning that are deeply embedded within artistic expression.

This exploration allows us to appreciate the multifaceted nature of human emotion and creativity, enriching our understanding of ourselves and the world around us in ways that are both enlightening and transformative. This exploration fosters a greater sense of empathy and insight, enabling us to connect more deeply with our individual journeys, evolving identities, and the shared experiences of humanity. In doing so, we enhance our collective understanding of life's complexities, forging connections that transcend time and culture and deepening our appreciation for the myriad ways in which art reflects and shapes human experience. It also serves as a bridge across generations and diverse cultures, highlighting the timeless relevance of these archetypes in contemporary society and encouraging us to engage more profoundly with the stories that define us. Through this engagement, we can better understand our place within the grand tapestry of life and the universal themes that bind us all together.

Feminine spirituality practices encompass a rich and diverse array of rituals and meditations, intricately weaving in artistic elements such as dance, painting, and song. These creative expressions not only serve as powerful gateways to honor the sacred feminine within each of us but also foster nurturing spaces that promote authenticity, introspection, and profound self-discovery. Engaging in these forms of creative expression allows us to delve into a much deeper understanding of our bodies, emotions, and spiritual selves, enabling us to connect with our essence on multiple levels.

Whether it's through painting a canvas that beautifully reflects our inner landscape or composing heartfelt lyrics that articulate our deepest truths and life experiences, these activities can lead to transformative healing and personal growth. By fully embracing our creativity, we tap into the abundant wellspring of feminine energy that nurtures our journeys and inspires our continuous evolution.

This journey not only enriches our individual lives but also cultivates a strong sense of community and interconnectedness. It encourages others to explore their unique paths of expression and discovery, creating a vibrant tapestry of shared experiences and insights. Through this collaborative spirit, we contribute to a collective awakening, where each individual's journey enhances the whole, fostering an environment that is ripe for collaboration, mutual support, and shared growth. In doing so, we celebrate the beauty of our individuality while recognizing the strength found in unity, creating a harmonious space for all to thrive

The relationship between the sacred feminine and the body is not only intricate but also profoundly essential, as women's health, fertility, and body image are deeply intertwined with our creative expressions in numerous and varied ways. Art and music serve as powerful vehicles for reclaiming our bodies and celebrating our unique, individual experiences, allowing for a rich and multifaceted exploration of identity and personal narrative. By authentically representing the struggles and triumphs of the feminine experience, artists create a meaningful dialogue that challenges societal norms and actively promotes body positivity in a world often rife with unrealistic standards and expectations.

This reclamation is vital in a culture that frequently seeks to diminish the power and beauty of the feminine form, often overlooking its inherent significance and value. Through various forms of creative expression, we not only empower ourselves but also uplift one another, creating a supportive community that encourages all women to embrace our bodies fully and honor them as sacred vessels worthy of love, respect, and celebration. By fostering this sense of solidarity and shared experience, we can inspire future generations to continue this vital conversation about the beauty and complexity of the feminine experience, ensuring that the richness of our narratives is recognized and celebrated in all its forms. In doing so, we pave the way for a more inclusive and compassionate understanding of what it means to be feminine in today's world.

In contemporary contexts, women continue to embody and express the sacred feminine through an intricate and vibrant tapestry of various artistic endeavors. They often skillfully blend traditional practices with modern themes and innovative approaches, creating a unique fusion that resonates with diverse audiences. The remarkable rise of female musicians, visual artists, performers, and creators, who draw deeply from their own unique experiences and rich cultural backgrounds, exemplifies this vibrant and dynamic expression of femininity. These extraordinary artists not only serve as powerful role models but also as inspirational figures, demonstrating that the sacred feminine is not just alive but also continuously evolving and adapting to the ever-changing world around us.

By celebrating their invaluable contributions to the arts, we not only elevate their voices and amplify their messages but also inspire a collective awakening to the profound beauty and strength that resides within each of us. In doing so, we recognize that their work serves as a mirror reflecting our shared experiences, emotions, and aspirations. In this way, art and music transform into not merely a celebration of the feminine spirit but also a compelling call to action, inviting us to embrace our own creative powers and express the sacred feminine in our everyday lives. This enriching process enhances our communities and fosters deeper connections among us all.

This vibrant movement encourages us to recognize the interconnectedness of our individual journeys and to support one another in the ongoing exploration of our identities, artistic expressions, and the myriad ways we can celebrate the sacred feminine together.

The Intersection of Feminism and Spirituality

The intersection of feminism and spirituality represents a profoundly powerful confluence that holds remarkable potential to transform not only individual lives but also the collective consciousness of women throughout our society in significant and lasting ways. At its core, feminism seeks to dismantle the entrenched patriarchal structures that have historically marginalized and oppressed women across various cultures and contexts. Meanwhile, spirituality offers a sacred and nurturing space for women to reconnect deeply with their inner selves and the divine presence that exists both within and around them, fostering a sense of wholeness and belonging. This unique synergy creates a holistic and multifaceted approach to empowerment, inviting women to explore the rich and profound sacred feminine as a source of unparalleled strength, wisdom, and inspiration that resonates deeply with their lived experiences.

As we immerse ourselves in this transformative intersection, we uncover the intricate and vibrant tapestry of goddess archetypes that can guide us on our personal and collective journeys. These archetypes serve not only as symbols of empowerment but also as mirrors reflecting the diverse aspects of the feminine experience. They provide both inspiration and a deep sense of belonging within a welcoming and supportive community that celebrates every woman's unique path. This exploration not only enriches our own lives but also contributes significantly to a broader cultural shift toward inclusivity, understanding, and a celebration of the diverse experiences of women everywhere. By recognizing the interconnectedness of our struggles and triumphs, we pave the way for a future that honors and uplifts all women's voices, fostering solidarity and mutual respect in our shared pursuit of justice and spiritual fulfillment.

Goddess archetypes serve as powerful and evocative symbols, representing the rich and intricate tapestry of attributes that women embody across an extensive array of cultures, traditions, and historical contexts. From the nurturing and life-giving essence of Gaia, who embodies the earth's fertility and sustains all forms of life, to the fierce independence and warrior spirit of Kali, who stands as an enduring symbol of empowerment, resilience, and transformation, these figures vividly remind us that the sacred feminine is not only multifaceted but also dynamic, fluid, and ever-evolving.

Exploring these archetypes allows women to delve into

profound depths of understanding, providing a richer and more nuanced perspective on their own strengths, vulnerabilities, and the unique narratives that shape their identities. This transformative process facilitates the creation of personal stories that honor both individual journeys and shared collective experiences as women, bridging generational gaps and fostering solidarity in the face of societal challenges that often seek to divide. Such exploration naturally evolves into a sacred practice, offering a dedicated space for profound reflection, insight, and revelation about how these archetypes resonate within our lives, influencing and shaping our identities in multifaceted and meaningful ways.

As we connect with the rich stories, timeless wisdom, and invaluable lessons of these goddesses, we can reclaim our inherent power, embrace our authentic selves, and redefine what it truly means to be a woman in today's complex, rapidly changing, and beautifully diverse world. This journey not only empowers individuals but also enriches communities, fostering a deeper appreciation for the sacred feminine in all its forms. It encourages a more inclusive understanding of womanhood, transcending boundaries and celebrating the diverse experiences and perspectives that women hold. By acknowledging and embracing this wide spectrum of feminine expression, we pave the way for greater unity and collaboration among women, creating a supportive environment that nurtures growth, healing, and empowerment for all. Together, we can cultivate a shared wisdom that uplifts each individual while honoring the collective strength of women everywhere, ensuring that the sacred feminine remains a vibrant and transformative force in our lives.

Feminine spirituality practices, which include rituals, meditations, and an array of sacred activities, provide meaningful and tangible ways to honor the sacred feminine in our daily lives. By engaging in ceremonies that celebrate not only the natural cycles of the earth and the phases of the moon but also personal milestones and significant life events, women can cultivate a deeper and more profound connection to the divine essence within themselves. These practices can be thoughtfully tailored to reflect individual beliefs, cultural backgrounds, and personal experiences, making them accessible, relatable, and relevant to women at various stages of life and spiritual journeys.

Through these transformative rituals, women can foster a strong sense of community, sharing their unique journeys and offering support to one another in their spiritual growth and exploration. This shared experience not only nurtures healing and understanding but also empowers women to embrace their unique paths and identities with confidence, strength, and grace. By actively participating in these enriching practices, women can celebrate their individuality while also connecting with the collective wisdom of the feminine spirit, thus creating a profound bond with others who share similar aspirations and experiences. This connection enhances their spiritual journeys, allowing them to navigate life with a sense of purpose and belonging.

Healing and empowerment are fundamental themes that beautifully intertwine at the intersection of feminism and spirituality, crafting a rich and intricate tapestry that invites deep exploration, reflection, and profound contemplation. By approaching both personal and collective healing through the lens of the sacred feminine, women are empowered to recognize not only the historical traumas that have profoundly shaped their lives but also to celebrate the remarkable resilience that has emerged from these often painful experiences. Techniques such as guided visualization, energy healing, and group sharing circles can significantly facilitate this transformative healing process, enabling women to reclaim their narratives and craft new stories that are deeply rooted in empowerment, self-affirmation, and a renewed sense of purpose and direction.

As we engage with the sacred feminine, we discover profound solace in the understanding that we are not alone in our struggles; rather, we are part of a vast and powerful lineage of women who have faced adversity, drawn strength from one another, and emerged even more robust, empowered, and united in our shared journey of healing, growth, and self-discovery. This collective experience not only enriches our individual paths but also weaves together a shared bond among women, fostering a sense of community and support that is essential for true healing.

In this sacred space, we learn to honor our unique journeys while celebrating the interconnectedness of all women, strengthening our resolve to uplift one another as we navigate the complexities of life together. As we delve deeper into our shared experiences, we cultivate a nurturing environment that encourages vulnerability and authenticity, allowing us to break free from the constraints of societal expectations. By acknowledging and embracing our collective strength, we empower ourselves and each other to forge new pathways, break cycles of trauma, and create lasting change within ourselves and our communities. This journey is not just about individual healing; it is a powerful movement towards collective empowerment, where every woman's story contributes to the rich tapestry of our shared human experience.

Exploring the intricate and multifaceted relationship between the sacred feminine and essential aspects of women's health, fertility, and body image is not merely important; it is an absolutely vital dimension of this profound intersection. As modern women navigate the pervasive societal pressures that continuously surround body image and health, the act of reconnecting with the sacred feminine emerges as an incredibly powerful antidote to these relentless challenges. By wholeheartedly embracing the innate wisdom of our bodies and joyfully celebrating our natural cycles, we can cultivate a much healthier, more nurturing, and compassionate relationship with ourselves and our experiences.

This reclamation of our bodies as sacred vessels empowers us to boldly challenge societal norms and redefine beauty according to our own authentic standards, rather than those that have been imposed upon us. In doing so, we not only honor our own unique journeys but also create a ripple effect that inspires and encourages countless other women to view their bodies and experiences as sacred, worthy of love, respect, and admiration. Through this transformative process, the intersection of feminism and spirituality evolves into a rich and multifaceted space for healing, growth, and empowerment. It invites women to rise as the goddesses they have always been and truly are, embracing their strength and divine qualities in a world that often seeks to diminish them.

This journey is not solely personal; it is a collective awakening that reinforces our inherent worth and the beauty of our shared experiences, fostering a profound sense of unity and connection among women everywhere. By engaging in this exploration, we actively contribute to a broader narrative that celebrates the sacred feminine, nurturing not just ourselves but also the generations of women who will follow in our footsteps. As we unite in this sacred purpose, we illuminate the path for future generations, ensuring that they, too, can embrace their divine essence and reclaim their power. Together, we can forge a new legacy that honors the sacred feminine, allowing it to flourish in a world that deeply needs its healing wisdom and strength.

Everyday Practices for Embracing the Divine

Embracing the divine in our everyday lives is a deeply transformative journey that invites us to reconnect with the sacred feminine, a vital essence that resides within each of us. There exists a variety of simple yet profoundly impactful rituals and habits designed specifically to empower women of all ages and stages in their lives as they honor and celebrate their inherent divinity. By thoughtfully integrating these meaningful practices into our daily routines, we can cultivate a richer, more profound awareness of the goddess archetypes that resonate deeply with our individual journeys and experiences. This enlightening process not only fosters a sense of empowerment and healing but also plays a crucial role in nurturing our spiritual growth and strengthening our connection to the divine feminine in all its beautiful forms. Engaging with these rituals invites us to honor our unique paths and recognize the sacred within ourselves and the world around us.

Embracing the divine can be powerfully achieved through the practice of ritual, which often serves as a deeply transformative experience that shapes our perceptions and connections in truly profound ways. Rituals need not always be grand or elaborate; they can be as simple yet deeply impactful as lighting a candle each morning, dedicating that sacred moment to a specific goddess or intention that resonates with immense meaning for you personally and spiritually.

Consider the myriad qualities embodied by different goddess figures from various cultures—such as the nurturing, life-giving energy of Demeter, who symbolizes growth, abundance, and the natural cycles of the earth, or the fierce, unwavering courage of Durga, who stands for strength, protection, and the ability to overcome adversity in the face of life's myriad challenges. By invoking these powerful archetypes in our rituals, we create a sacred space that honors their attributes while simultaneously enabling us to manifest these empowering qualities in our daily lives, infusing our routines with intention, love, and reverence.

These rituals serve as profound reminders of our intrinsic connection to the divine and the immense strength that resides within each of us, guiding us through our journey and helping us cultivate resilience, purpose, and a deeper understanding of ourselves and our place within the vast universe. Engaging in these meaningful practices can greatly enrich our spiritual lives, enhance our sense of belonging to a greater whole, and foster a deeper appreciation for the interconnectedness of all beings. This illumination of our paths inspires us to live with intention, mindfulness, and awareness in every moment, reminding us of the sacredness present in the ordinary as we navigate our journeys.

Meditation is an extraordinarily accessible and deeply transformative practice, serving as a powerful means to connect with the sacred feminine energy that resides within each of us. By setting aside just a few moments each day for stillness and reflection, individuals can significantly unlock pathways to inner wisdom, self-discovery, and profound healing. Engaging in guided meditations that emphasize themes such as femininity, empowerment, and self-love can be especially transformative, enriching the lives of those who are navigating their unique journeys of growth and understanding. Visualizing oneself surrounded by the nurturing and loving energy of the divine can greatly enhance body positivity and acceptance, encouraging women to embrace and strengthen their relationships with their bodies. This practice not only cultivates a deeper sense of self-awareness but also fosters a supportive community where individuals can share their experiences and insights, thereby amplifying the transformative effects of meditation on their overall well-being and personal evolution. This practice nurtures a deep sense of self-love and appreciation, fostering a profound understanding of the sacred feminine as a lasting source of strength, resilience, and inspiration to draw upon during life's challenges. This journey promotes a holistic approach to well-being and personal growth, empowering individuals to embrace their most authentic selves and live their truth. Through meditation, they can navigate life's complexities with grace, confidence, and a strong sense of purpose, turning challenges into valuable opportunities for growth and self-realization. Such transformative practices not only uplift the individual but also create a positive ripple effect in their surroundings, cultivating a vibrant community rooted in love, mutual support, and shared aspirations for wellness. This interconnectedness enriches the meditation experience, inviting deeper connections and collective healing, thus enhancing the journey for all involved

Engaging with nature is not only an essential but also a transformative aspect of fully embracing the divine essence within us. Whether it's walking barefoot in the lush, cool grass that cushions our steps, tending lovingly to a vibrant, flourishing garden that bursts with life, or simply taking a moment to observe the ever-changing, breathtaking seasons that unfold around us, connecting deeply with the earth can profoundly ground us in our feminine essence.

Consider forming a nature-based spiritual practice, such as moon rituals that honor the sacred cycles of the moon, which are intricately woven into the rich fabric of feminine spirituality and reflect our deepest connections to the cosmos. These rituals and practices serve as powerful reminders that we are an integral part of a larger cycle encompassing life, death, and rebirth, echoing the timeless rhythms of nature itself. This beautifully resonates with the myths and legends that have celebrated the sacred feminine throughout the ages and across diverse cultures.

These stories not only highlight our profound connection to the Earth and to each other, but they also guide us as we navigate our unique spiritual journeys, reminding us that we are never alone in this sacred dance of existence. As we immerse ourselves in nature's beauty, we open ourselves to the wisdom it offers, deepening our understanding of ourselves and the universe in which we reside.

Embracing the divine is ultimately a journey that is not only deeply personal but also profoundly collective in nature, intertwining the individual with the communal. By sharing our diverse stories, rich experiences, and varied spiritual practices with one another—especially among women—we can cultivate a powerful sense of community that enriches our lives in truly meaningful and transformative ways. Whether through intimate circles that foster deep connections, engaging workshops that spark creativity and insight, or vibrant online platforms that bridge distances, these connections create invaluable spaces for healing, empowerment, and mutual support.

By celebrating the rich multiplicity of goddess archetypes alongside the myriad expressions of the sacred feminine in our contemporary lives, we honor our individuality while simultaneously strengthening the bonds that unite us as a collective force of love and creativity. Together, we can rise as a unified force, honoring the divine essence that exists within ourselves and one another. In doing so, we create a ripple effect of love, strength, and transformation that resonates deeply throughout the world around us, inspiring others to join in this uplifting journey and contributing to a larger movement of empowerment.

Through our shared commitment to this path, we can foster a greater understanding and appreciation for the sacred feminine, igniting a vibrant movement that echoes through time and space, inviting all to partake in this transformative experience of growth and learning. As we nurture these connections, we empower ourselves and each other to explore the depths of our spiritual journeys, weaving together a rich tapestry of wisdom and resilience that uplifts our communities. This collective effort not only enriches our shared human experience but also lays the groundwork for profound and lasting impacts in our lives and the lives of others. Each connection we forge adds to this tapestry, creating an enduring legacy of love, strength, and shared purpose that reverberates far beyond our immediate circles, transforming the world around us in meaningful ways.

The Sacred Feminine and Men

The concept of the sacred feminine encompasses a rich and diverse range of qualities, energies, and archetypes that have traditionally been associated with femininity. These include essential traits such as intuition, nurturing, compassion, and creativity, which are often celebrated in women. However, this idea extends beyond gender boundaries; it holds significant relevance for men as well. By embracing the principles of the sacred feminine, men can gain deeper insights into their own identities and enhance their understanding of relationships with others, fostering a more holistic approach to personal growth and connection.

Men who engage with the sacred feminine often find themselves embarking on a truly remarkable journey, one that profoundly deepens their connection to their own emotional landscapes and vulnerabilities. This journey opens expansive new doors to self-discovery and personal growth that they may have never previously envisioned or even considered possible. By actively embracing qualities that are frequently labeled as feminine—such as compassion, intuition, empathy, and nurturing—they can cultivate a significantly heightened sense of empathy. This not only dramatically enhances their emotional intelligence but also fosters healthier, more meaningful relationships with others in their lives, enriching their interactions on multiple levels.

This transformative journey encourages men to break free from the constraints of societal expectations and norms that impose rigid definitions of masculinity. It allows them to embrace a more holistic and authentic expression of self, one that genuinely reflects their true essence and individuality. Such exploration not only enriches their personal lives but also contributes to a more balanced and nuanced understanding of gender dynamics in society as a whole. As men delve deeply into these often overlooked aspects of their being, they may discover a newfound attunement to their own feelings and experiences. This heightened awareness also enables them to connect more deeply with the emotional experiences of those around them, creating a ripple effect that strengthens their relationships.

This journey leads to the development of stronger communities and deeper bonds with others, fostering a profound sense of unity and shared understanding among diverse individuals. This ongoing process can facilitate a significant and transformative shift in perspective, empowering men to appreciate the true value of vulnerability and encouraging them to embrace their full humanity. Such empowerment can have far-reaching ripple effects in their interactions and relationships, fostering a vibrant culture of understanding, compassion, and mutual respect that benefits everyone involved. In doing so, they contribute to a richer social fabric that nurtures growth and connection among individuals from all walks of life, enhancing the overall well-being of their communities.

The sacred feminine serves as a vital counterbalance to the traditional masculine archetype, which often emphasizes qualities such as strength, stoicism, and dominance. By embracing and integrating various aspects of the sacred feminine, men can embark on a transformative journey toward discovering a more harmonious and balanced way of being. This approach honors not only their inherent strength but also their emotional sensitivity and vulnerability. By fostering this deeper balance, men can cultivate greater harmony within themselves, enriching their interactions with others. This enriched perspective promotes healthier relationships that beautifully reflect both power and compassion, leading to a more fulfilling and connected existence.

The concept of the sacred feminine invites men to engage in a much deeper and more meaningful exploration of their relationships with women. It encourages them to delve into the rich and complex feminine aspects that reside within themselves, fostering a genuine appreciation for the nuances, subtleties, and intricacies of these qualities. This approach underscores the critical importance of nurturing profound respect for the unique experiences of women, while recognizing their invaluable contributions to society, which have so often been overlooked, undervalued, or dismissed throughout the course of history. By embracing this perspective, we not only promote a sense of partnership and collaboration but also actively work against the unnecessary competition or conflict that has historically existed between the genders.

Cultivating this heightened awareness and appreciation can lead to healthier, more fulfilling dynamics, not just in personal relationships but also within workplaces and society at large. This transformative process paves the way for a more harmonious coexistence that benefits everyone involved, allowing for richer interactions and deeper connections that transcend superficial boundaries and societal expectations. When we fully embrace the sacred feminine, we create an environment where mutual understanding, respect, and support can truly flourish and thrive.

This approach fosters a vibrant community that not only celebrates diversity but also nurtures personal and collective growth on multiple levels, enriching the lives of all individuals within it. The journey toward recognizing and honoring the sacred feminine serves as a powerful catalyst for change. It encourages a more inclusive, compassionate, and equitable world for everyone, where each voice is not only heard but also valued. By embracing these ideals, we can initiate a profound cultural shift that recognizes the importance of the sacred feminine in shaping a future that is just, harmonious, and filled with opportunities for all.

The sacred feminine transcends the idea of diminishing masculinity in any way; instead, it is fundamentally about enriching and enhancing it in profound and deeply meaningful ways. Men who fully embrace this transformative concept can uncover new, exciting, and transformative pathways to personal growth, emotional depth, and the ability to forge meaningful connections with others. This journey not only fosters their own development and understanding but also significantly contributes to the creation of a more inclusive, compassionate, and harmonious world for everyone involved. It paves the way for deeper, more authentic relationships, fostering a greater sense of community and belonging. By engaging with the sacred feminine, men can explore dimensions of their identity that allow them to connect with others on a more profound level, enriching their lives and the lives of those around them.

Living the Sacred Feminine in Our Relationships with Men

Stepping into the sacred feminine in our relationships with men is a transformative journey that involves embracing and fully integrating qualities traditionally associated with the feminine, such as intuition, nurturing, compassion, and receptivity. This embodiment transcends mere adherence to societal stereotypes; it is fundamentally about reclaiming, honoring, and celebrating the true essence of femininity in all its forms. By actively engaging with these qualities, we create a dynamic that fosters balance, harmony, and mutual respect in our relationships. This nurturing environment allows both partners to not only thrive but also to grow individually and collectively, deepening their connection and understanding in a supportive and enriching manner

Women can embody the sacred feminine by wholeheartedly embracing authenticity and vulnerability in every aspect of their lives. By openly sharing their true selves—expressing their deepest desires, fears, and dreams—they not only create a welcoming and inclusive space but also encourage others to do the same. This openness fosters deeper connections and understanding among those around them, enriching their relationships in profound ways. It invites men to respond with their own authenticity, cultivating a mutual atmosphere of respect and comprehension that benefits everyone involved, creating a tapestry of shared experiences and emotions.

By tapping into their intuition and actively cultivating emotional awareness, women can skillfully guide their relationships with sensitivity and insight, navigating the often complex and intricate dynamics of human connection. Trusting their feelings and instincts empowers them to effectively address challenges and obstacles, enhancing communication and fostering a dynamic that is both supportive and empathetic. This nurturing approach not only enriches their own lives but also positively influences those they care about.

Embodying the sacred feminine often involves nurturing not just others but also oneself, recognizing that self-care is essential for healthy relationships. By wholeheartedly supporting their partners in pursuing their ambitions and dreams while simultaneously tending to their own needs and aspirations, women create a balanced and harmonious relationship where both individuals can flourish and thrive together. This synergy enhances their shared journey in profound and meaningful ways, allowing each person to grow, evolve, and contribute positively to the partnership. It is essential that both partners recognize the importance of self-care and mutual support, as this strong foundation not only solidifies their bond but also enhances the overall quality of their connection, fostering a relationship that is resilient, joyful, and deeply connected.

A vital aspect of the sacred feminine is the essential ability to set and maintain healthy boundaries. Women can embody this principle by clearly and assertively communicating their limits and expectations, which allows for mutual respect and understanding within the relationship. Establishing and honoring boundaries is crucial, as it creates a safe and nurturing space for both partners to express themselves freely and authentically. This environment fosters genuine emotional connections that are fundamental to a thriving partnership.

Embracing the sacred feminine also involves a deep appreciation for and celebration of the masculine qualities found in men. Recognizing the valuable strengths that men bring to a relationship—such as their courage, protectiveness, determination, and resilience—fosters a sense of partnership and collaboration rather than competition. By valuing these qualities, women can encourage a harmonious dynamic that nurtures both individuals, allowing each partner to flourish while supporting one another's growth.

Women can further embody the sacred feminine by actively creating and nurturing opportunities for meaningful connection and intimacy. This might involve thoughtfully planning activities that encourage bonding—such as shared hobbies, engaging in deep and insightful conversations, or simply dedicating quality time to spend together in a relaxed and enjoyable manner. Such intentional efforts serve to strengthen the emotional ties that bind partners, enhancing the overall quality of the relationship. This, in turn, creates a deeper sense of unity, trust, and understanding, enriching the journey they share together and laying a strong foundation for lasting love and fulfillment.

Relationships are often put to the test by misunderstandings, conflicts, and the inevitable challenges that life presents. Embracing the sacred feminine requires a profound and unwavering commitment to practicing forgiveness and compassion. It is essential to recognize that both partners are inherently human, each possessing their own unique imperfections and vulnerabilities. This nurturing attitude not only aids in healing emotional wounds but also fosters significant personal and relational growth over time, creating a deeper bond between partners. The essence of the sacred feminine is intricately linked to creativity and the spirit of playfulness. Engaging in creative activities together—whether through art, music, shared hobbies, or simply infusing a sense of play into everyday interactions—can tremendously enhance joy and spontaneity within the relationship. Such playful engagement serves as a beautiful reminder of the profound joy found in shared experiences, reinforcing the deep connection between partners.

To truly embody the sacred feminine, one must strive for a harmonious balance within the relationship. This balance involves acknowledging and valuing the importance of both feminine and masculine energies, allowing each partner to express these qualities freely, authentically, and without fear of judgment or reprisal. A balanced relationship not only nurtures individual growth but also cultivates mutual respect and understanding. This creates a supportive environment where both partners can thrive together, exploring the depths of their connection and enriching one another's lives in meaningful ways. It is through this dynamic interplay of energies and the commitment to growth that relationships can flourish and evolve, overcoming obstacles and celebrating the beauty of unity.

By fully stepping into these essential aspects of the sacred feminine, women have the remarkable opportunity to cultivate relationships that are not only deeply fulfilling but also profoundly transformative in numerous ways. This whole life, whole being approach not only fosters deeper connections but also encourages mutual growth and understanding alongside their male partners. Engaging in this meaningful journey invites both individuals to honor and appreciate their unique strengths, perspectives, and contributions to the relationship. By doing so, they can build a partnership that is firmly grounded in love, respect, and a deep understanding of one another's needs and aspirations, leading to a richer and more harmonious union.

Sacred Feminine and the Body

Understanding the Body as Sacred

In the transformative journey toward fully embracing the sacred feminine, one of the most profound realizations we can arrive at is recognizing our bodies as sacred vessels, imbued with deep meaning and purpose that extends far beyond the surface. This understanding transcends mere physicality; it encompasses the spirit, emotions, and the very essence of who we are as women, reflecting our unique experiences, identities, and the intricate stories we carry within us, often shaped by our relationships, cultures, and environments. Throughout the rich tapestry of history, various cultures have revered the female body, frequently associating it with the natural cycles of life, fertility, and the powerful, life-giving forces of the Earth itself, which remind us of our interconnectedness with nature. By honoring our bodies as sacred, we not only reclaim our inherent power but also acknowledge and celebrate the deep wisdom they hold within us, recognizing that our bodies are repositories of knowledge, resilience, and strength. This profound reverence allows us to cultivate a richer, more meaningful connection to our true selves, empowering us to navigate the complexities of the world with grace, authenticity, and a renewed sense of purpose that resonates deeply within our being. Embracing this sacred understanding invites us to celebrate our femininity in all its diverse forms and fosters a deeper appreciation for the shared experiences of womanhood, creating a sense of unity and sisterhood among us as we journey together, supporting and uplifting one another in our collective quest for empowerment and fulfillment.

As we embrace the sacred feminine, we embark on a transformative journey that reveals the profound depths of our existence. One of the most enlightening realizations during this process is the recognition that our bodies serve as sacred vessels, filled with deep meaning and purpose that extends far beyond what meets the eye. This understanding transcends the surface of physicality; it encompasses our spirit, our emotions, and the very essence of our identities as women, reflecting the unique experiences we each carry, along with the intricate stories shaped by our relationships, cultures, and environments. Throughout the rich tapestry of human history, diverse cultures have revered the female body, often associating it with the natural cycles of life, fertility, and the potent, life-giving forces of the Earth itself, reminding us of our profound interconnectedness with nature and all living beings. By honoring our bodies as sacred entities, we not only reclaim our inherent power but also acknowledge and celebrate the profound wisdom they hold within us. Our bodies become repositories of knowledge, resilience, and strength, embodying our journeys and experiences. This deep reverence empowers us to cultivate a richer, more meaningful connection to our true selves, allowing us to navigate the complexities of life with grace and authenticity. We gain a renewed sense of purpose that resonates deeply within our being. Embracing this sacred understanding invites us to celebrate our femininity in its myriad forms, fostering a deeper appreciation for the shared experiences of womanhood. This creates a sense of unity and sisterhood among us as we journey together, supporting and uplifting one another in our collective quest for empowerment, fulfillment, and a deeper connection to the sacred feminine within us all.

The body, with its myriad diverse forms and expressions, serves as an extraordinarily significant site of divine expression and connection, brimming with profound meaning and purpose. Each curve, scar, and mark intricately narrates a unique and powerful story of resilience, growth, and transformation, reflecting the complex and intricate journey of life itself in ways that are as varied as the individuals who inhabit these bodies. Goddess archetypes from a multitude of cultures vividly illuminate this deep connection—whether it's the nurturing embrace of Gaia, symbolizing the earth's abundant life and interconnectedness; the fierce warrior spirit of Durga, representing unwavering strength and courage in the face of adversity; the compassionate healing presence of Kuan Yin, invoking the essence of mercy and compassion for all beings; or the wise and protective nature of Artemis, embodying independence and fierce protectiveness over those she cares for. These powerful and revered figures serve as profound reminders of the rich tapestry of diverse experiences of femininity and the immense strength that lies within them, emphasizing the myriad ways women can embody these qualities in their own lives and communities, transcending cultural boundaries and societal expectations.

By embracing these archetypes, we cultivate a deeper appreciation for our bodies, viewing them not merely as objects to be scrutinized or judged, but as sacred temples that embody our unique journeys and the collective wisdom of womanhood throughout history and across cultures. In doing this, we honor our individuality and personal narratives, while also recognizing the shared experiences that unite us all, fostering a profound sense of community and connection among women everywhere. This encourages solidarity and mutual support as we celebrate our unique paths, the beauty of our shared experiences, and the transformative power of our collective stories. It invites us to uplift one another as we navigate the complexities of life together, weaving a narrative of empowerment, understanding, and love that resonates across generations. We ensure that the voices of women—past, present, and future—continue to be heard and celebrated in all their diversity and depth, transforming our understanding of what it means to be a woman in today's world. Such an approach not only honors our past but also paves the way for future generations, enriching the cultural landscape with stories of strength, resilience, and beauty.

Feminine spirituality practices invite us to engage with our bodies in intentional and nurturing ways, encouraging a deep and profound connection that goes well beyond the surface. Rituals that celebrate our natural cycles, honor our inherent sensuality, and promote essential self-care are absolutely vital in fostering a meaningful and enriching relationship with our physical selves. Activities such as meditation, breathwork, and movement can significantly facilitate a deeper understanding of how our bodies respond to various emotions and life experiences, allowing for a more nuanced awareness of our internal landscapes. Engaging in these transformative practices not only empowers us to release negative beliefs and patterns that we may unconsciously hold about our bodies, but it also creates the much-needed space for healing, renewal, and personal transformation. As we cultivate this sacred relationship with ourselves, we open doors to empowerment and personal growth, recognizing more profoundly that our bodies are not merely vessels but powerful conduits of energy, intuition, and wisdom that guide us through our journeys in life. By nurturing this connection, we honor our true selves and embrace the fullness of our experiences.

The myths and legends that celebrate the sacred feminine often highlight a profound and intricate connection between women and their bodies. These timeless stories of goddesses embodying strength, wisdom, and grace provide a powerful framework for understanding our own diverse experiences. These narratives can serve not only as tools for personal reflection but also as gateways to deeper understanding, encouraging us to explore and confront our beliefs surrounding body image, health, and fertility in a more meaningful way. By delving into these rich myths, we can uncover the archetypal energies that resonate deeply within us, allowing for a richer, more nuanced comprehension of our bodies as sacred entities intricately intertwined with the spiritual realm and the universe at large.

In our contemporary world, women are increasingly reclaiming their bodies as sacred spaces, skillfully navigating societal expectations and pressures with both grace and resilience. Through a foundation of community support, the sharing of personal stories, and the powerful momentum of empowerment movements, women are actively redefining beauty, health, and wellness on their own terms. By celebrating the sacred feminine in our lives, we honor not only ourselves but also the rich lineage of women who have come before us, paving the way with their strength and wisdom. As we continue to explore and fully embrace the sacredness of our bodies, we contribute to a collective healing that honors the divine feminine within all women. This journey fosters a profound sense of unity and empowerment that transcends generations, creating a ripple effect that inspires future generations to honor their own sacredness and individuality. Together, we are not just reclaiming our bodies, but also reshaping the narrative around womanhood, instilling a deeper understanding of our worth and the beauty inherent in our experiences.

Fertility, Health, and Wellness Practices

First, we must recognize that when we discuss the concept of the sacred feminine, the term fertility extends far beyond mere childbearing. It encompasses a broader understanding of creation and manifestation. Anything we cultivate, bring into existence, or nurture to flourish is a profound expression of fertility in its many forms

Fertility, health, and wellness are not only profound aspects of the sacred feminine but are also intricately woven into the rich tapestry of women's lives across a multitude of cultures and throughout the ages. In our exploration of the divine feminine, we can draw deeply upon the timeless wisdom of goddess archetypes that embody the dual principles of fertility and healing, resonating with women from diverse backgrounds and traditions. Take, for instance, the nurturing and abundant qualities of Demeter, who represents the harvest and symbolizes the deep, nurturing bond between mother and child. Her essence serves as a powerful reminder of the fundamental connection that sustains life itself and nourishes our very existence. In contrast, the transformative and fierce energy of Kali signifies both destruction and rebirth, illustrating the powerful cycles that define our existence and the intrinsic balance between creation and dissolution.

These influential figures serve as poignant reminders of the cyclical nature of life and the incredible power inherent in our bodies as women. They stand as enduring symbols of our innate ability to create, nurture, and heal, echoing through the ages and across cultures. By celebrating our unique journeys as women, we honor the profound changes that accompany each stage of life, recognizing the beauty in both creation and transformation. Each phase brings its own wisdom, challenges, and joys, enriching our understanding of what it means to walk this path as women. By wholeheartedly embracing these multifaceted aspects of our existence, we can cultivate a deeper and more meaningful connection to ourselves and to the broader feminine experience that unites us all in our shared humanity.

In acknowledging and celebrating the rich diversity of women's experiences, we empower one another and reinforce the sacred feminine, understanding that our collective stories contribute to a greater and more nuanced understanding of what it truly means to be a woman in this world. Together, we can inspire a greater appreciation for the intricate web of life that connects us all, weaving our individual narratives into the broader tapestry of womanhood and highlighting the strength, resilience, and beauty that define us as a community. By fostering this sense of unity, we create a supportive environment where every woman can thrive, celebrate her journey, and contribute her voice to the ever-evolving story of womanhood.

Integrating health and wellness practices into our daily lives is essential for truly honoring the sacred feminine. This integration can encompass a variety of rituals that help connect us more profoundly to our bodies and the earth, including moon ceremonies, herbal healing, and mindful movement exercises. By actively engaging in enriching practices such as yoga, dance, or meditation, we can cultivate a deeper awareness of our bodies, enhancing both our physical and spiritual health. These activities not only promote individual wellness but also foster a strong sense of community among women, as we come together to support and uplift one another in our shared journeys toward holistic well-being. In doing so, we create a nurturing environment that allows us to flourish, embrace our femininity, and empower each other in our pursuit of balance and harmony.

Meditation and mindfulness practices that are deeply rooted in feminine spirituality provide a powerful avenue for both healing and empowerment. These practices invite women to engage with their inner worlds and cultivate a sense of connection to the divine. Visualization techniques that invoke the energy of various goddesses can significantly aid women in harnessing their inner strength and creativity. For example, meditating on the serene image of a nurturing goddess can offer profound comfort and solace during challenging times, while invoking the fierce and dynamic energy of a warrior goddess can inspire not just courage but also decisive action. Each meditation session can serve as a vital reminder of the divine power that resides within us all, encouraging us to fully embrace our authentic selves and to celebrate the unique gifts and talents we possess. Through these practices, women can foster a deeper sense of self-awareness and empowerment, transforming their lives and the lives of those around them.

The relationship between the sacred feminine and women's health is further illuminated through the rich and intricate lens of mythology. Myths often depict powerful and dynamic female figures who navigate the complex and multifaceted realities of fertility, motherhood, and healing. These narratives reflect the diverse experiences that women encounter across various cultures and generations. By immersing ourselves in these timeless and resonant stories, we can gain profound insights into our own lives, recognizing the universal themes of resilience, transformation, and empowerment that resonate across time. Such narratives serve as vital and uplifting reminders that we are not alone in our struggles and triumphs; they connect us to a much larger tapestry of feminine experience that spans both time and space. This connection provides a wellspring of inspiration, comfort, and strength, encouraging us to embrace our journeys while honoring the collective wisdom of women throughout history. By engaging with these stories, we not only celebrate our individuality but also the shared heritage that binds us all together, enriching our understanding of ourselves and the world around us.

In modern contexts, women embody the sacred feminine in a variety of diverse and profoundly meaningful ways. From advocating fiercely for reproductive rights to creating inclusive spaces for holistic health and wellness, contemporary women are reclaiming their inherent power and redefining the concept of wellness on their own unique terms. By embracing our distinct paths and honoring our bodies in their entirety, we can forge deep connections with one another that transcend both time and cultural boundaries. Together, we have the potential to grow a collective healing that not only honors the sacred feminine but also empowers us to rise as goddesses in our own right. In this journey, we celebrate the immense beauty and intricate complexity of our individual and collective journeys through life, fostering a supportive community that uplifts and inspires.

Body Image and the Journey to Acceptance

In our journey toward embracing the sacred feminine, one of the most profound challenges we often encounter is our relationship with body image. This journey extends far beyond mere aesthetics; it is intricately connected to how we perceive ourselves and our inherent worth in a world that frequently promotes unrealistic and unattainable ideals. The sacred feminine calls us to reconnect with our bodies as sacred vessels, deserving of unwavering love and profound respect, irrespective of societal pressures and norms. Through this exploration, we can learn to honor our unique shapes, sizes, and forms as beautiful and powerful expressions of the divine. By cultivating this deeper understanding, we can transform our self-relationship and foster a greater sense of acceptance and celebration of our individuality.

Throughout history, a multitude of goddess archetypes has provided us with a rich and vibrant tapestry of body positivity and self-acceptance. From the nurturing, voluptuous curves of Venus to the fierce, unyielding strength of Kali, these divine figures embody a wide array of aspects of femininity that celebrate the body in all its beautiful manifestations. By delving into the stories and attributes of these goddesses, we can glean invaluable wisdom on embracing our unique individuality and recognizing the profound beauty inherent in our differences. Each goddess acts as a mirror, reflecting the vast multiplicity of the feminine experience, while also urging us to reclaim our own personal narratives. This process fosters a deeper sense of acceptance and love for our bodies as they are, encouraging us to appreciate our unique forms and experiences in a world that often imposes narrow definitions of beauty.

Body image and sacred femininity are profoundly intertwined concepts that significantly shape how women perceive themselves and their bodies, particularly in relation to a diverse array of cultural, spiritual, and personal beliefs. Historically, across numerous societies and epochs, the female body has been both venerated and objectified, leading to a complex and often intricate relationship with self-image that varies across different contexts. This multifaceted dynamic can have a substantial and lasting impact on women's mental and emotional well-being, influencing how they navigate their identities and experiences in a world that frequently presents conflicting and often contradictory messages about beauty, desirability, and self-worth. The interplay between societal standards and individual beliefs can create considerable challenges, as women strive to reconcile their self-perceptions with external expectations and pressures. This ongoing struggle shapes their journeys toward self-acceptance, empowerment, and a deeper understanding of their own worth beyond societal norms.

Female beauty standards have evolved significantly over time, influenced by cultural, social, and economic factors. Historically, these standards have often been shaped by patriarchal norms, leading to a narrow definition of what constitutes beauty. The concept of the male gaze is something now pervasive in our culture. It highlights how visual arts and literature often reflect and reinforce a masculine perspective, objectifying women and framing their beauty in a way that caters to male desire. This dynamic can lead to women feeling pressured to conform to specific ideals, which are frequently unrealistic and unattainable.

In contemporary society, beauty standards continue to be perpetuated through media, advertising, and social platforms, where images of idealized femininity are ubiquitous. These standards often emphasize physical attributes such as youth, slimness, and particular facial features, creating a narrow archetype of beauty that many women feel compelled to strive for. This pursuit can result in various psychological impacts, including body dissatisfaction, low self-esteem, and even eating disorders.

The concept of sacred femininity offers a counter-narrative to these limiting beauty standards. It emphasizes the intrinsic value of femininity beyond physical appearance, celebrating qualities such as intuition, compassion, creativity, and strength. Sacred femininity encourages women to embrace their diverse identities and experiences, challenging the notion that their worth is tied solely to their looks. This perspective promotes a holistic understanding of beauty that encompasses emotional and spiritual well-being.

In recent years, there has been a growing movement towards redefining beauty standards, driven by body positivity, inclusivity, and empowerment. This shift seeks to dismantle the male gaze by advocating for representations of women that reflect their true selves and diverse experiences. By embracing sacred femininity, women can reclaim their narratives, fostering a sense of self-worth that is not contingent upon external validation or societal expectations. We are all beautiful.

The intersection of female beauty standards, the male gaze, and the concept of sacred femininity underscores the urgent need for a more inclusive and empowering understanding of what it truly means to be beautiful in today's society. This intersectionality calls for a vibrant celebration of the multifaceted nature of femininity, where women from all walks of life are encouraged to redefine and embrace their own unique beauty on their own terms. It emphasizes the importance of breaking free from the constraints of traditional norms and societal expectations, allowing for a richer and more diverse portrayal of beauty that honors individual experiences and identities.

Sacred femininity refers to the recognition and celebration of the feminine divine within women. It emphasizes the inherent value of femininity, encouraging women to embrace their bodies as sacred vessels filled with potential, creativity, and power. This perspective invites women to honor their bodies in all forms, recognizing that each shape, size, and feature tells a unique story and reflects a deeper truth about their identity.

The pressure to conform to societal beauty standards often distorts body image, leading to pervasive feelings of inadequacy and self-doubt among individuals. However, embracing the concept of sacred femininity invites a profound shift in focus from seeking external validation to nurturing internal acceptance. This perspective encourages women to view their bodies as powerful embodiments of life and strength, deserving of love, respect, and appreciation regardless of societal expectations and pressures. By fostering this mindset, women can cultivate a deep sense of self-worth that transcends superficial ideals.

Practicing self-love and embracing body positivity can be viewed as powerful acts of reclaiming the sacred essence of femininity. This journey often involves engaging in a variety of practices that nurture the body and spirit, such as yoga, dance, or meditation, all of which help foster a deeper and more meaningful connection to oneself. By cultivating a genuine appreciation for the body's incredible capabilities and strengths, rather than fixating solely on external appearance, women can discover a profound sense of personal power and pride in their femininity, leading to greater confidence and self-acceptance.

Additionally, sacred femininity not only promotes the powerful idea of sisterhood but also emphasizes the importance of shared experiences among women. This fosters a nurturing and supportive community that actively uplifts and affirms one another. By coming together in this way, women can harness their collective strength, which serves to counteract the isolating effects of negative body image. This sense of unity and support is essential in fostering resilience, helping each individual to navigate and overcome personal challenges.

The journey toward cultivating a positive body image through the profound lens of sacred femininity involves wholeheartedly embracing authenticity, joyfully celebrating individuality, and deeply recognizing the divine essence that resides within every woman. This journey is a powerful call to honor and cherish the body as a sacred space, one that is truly worthy of love, acceptance, and profound reverence, encouraging women to connect with their innate worth and beauty.

Embracing the sacred feminine also involves engaging in a variety of feminine spirituality practices that deeply nurture our connection to our bodies. Rituals such as dance, yoga, and meditation not only allow us to inhabit our bodies fully but also foster a profound sense of empowerment and self-acceptance. As we actively engage in these enriching practices, we create sacred spaces where we can freely explore our feelings about our bodies without any judgment or fear. This ongoing journey of self-discovery is essential as it helps us cultivate a deeper understanding of our physical forms. It allows us to truly appreciate their inherent strength and resilience, especially as they navigate the numerous challenges life presents. By honoring our bodies through these rituals, we embrace the fullness of our being, celebrating each aspect of ourselves in a holistic manner.

Healing and empowerment are fundamental components of our relationship with body image, shaping how we perceive ourselves in a world full of contrasting messages. The journey toward acceptance often necessitates a courageous confrontation with deeply ingrained beliefs and pervasive societal messages that insist we are not enough as we are. Through various techniques such as visualization and guided meditations, we can actively begin to dismantle these limiting beliefs, replacing them with powerful affirmations that reinforce our inherent worth and uniqueness. In this nurturing healing space, we take the time to honor the profound wisdom of our bodies, acknowledging the rich stories they carry and the diverse journeys they have undertaken throughout our lives. By embracing this practice, we empower ourselves to stand firmly in our own truths, celebrating the sacred feminine energy that resides within each of us, allowing it to shine brightly and authentically.

As we navigate the complexities of modern life, the sacred feminine continues to reveal itself in our body image journeys. By embodying the principles of the sacred feminine, we can forge a path of acceptance and love, not only for ourselves but for all women. This collective journey towards embracing our bodies can spark a broader movement of body positivity, encouraging others to celebrate their individuality and the unique expressions of the feminine divine. In this way, the journey to acceptance becomes not just personal but a shared celebration of our sacred selves, inspiring future generations to honor the goddess within.

Movement and Dance as Spiritual Expression

Movement and dance have long been acknowledged as profoundly impactful forms of spiritual expression, especially within the context of the sacred feminine. For women across a multitude of cultures and traditions, the act of moving the body transcends mere physicality; it evolves into a sacred practice that forges a deep connection between the spirit and the earth, the divine, and the very essence of femininity itself. This subchapter explores how movement and dance function as essential manifestations of the Goddess archetypes. Through this exploration, women are empowered to embody a diverse array of aspects of the sacred feminine, enabling them to tap into deeper layers of empowerment, healing, and self-discovery.

Throughout history, goddesses have been associated with movement and rhythm, each embodying unique attributes that resonate with the feminine experience. Terpsichore, one of the nine Muses in Greek mythology, is revered as the goddess of dance and the art of movement. Her name, which means delight in the dance, encapsulates her essence as a source of inspiration for all forms of dance. As a Muse, she embodies the joy, creativity, and expression found in physical movement, serving as a bridge between the divine and the earthly through the rhythm of the body.

In the context of the sacred feminine, Terpsichore represents the celebration of the body as a vessel for spiritual expression and connection. The sacred feminine encompasses qualities such as intuition, nurturing, and the embodiment of life, and Terpsichore's influence is intricately tied to these themes. Dance, as an art form, allows individuals to connect with their inner selves and the cosmos, transcending the mundane and entering a space where the spiritual and physical converge.

The act of dancing, especially in sacred rituals, has historically been a means of honoring the divine feminine. It allows for a physical manifestation of reverence, where movement becomes a prayer or an offering. Terpsichore, as the Muse of dance, encourages this sacred expression, inviting individuals to explore their bodies, celebrate their femininity, and connect with the rhythms of the natural world. This connection is vital in recognizing the power of the feminine spirit, which has often been marginalized or suppressed in various cultures.

Through the lens of Terpsichore, the ancient muse of dance, we can perceive dance not merely as a form of artistic expression but as a powerful transformative practice that empowers individuals to reclaim their bodies and authentically express their unique identities. This captivating art form serves as a profound reminder of the divine nature inherent in movement and the immense joy that arises from fully inhabiting and embracing one's physical being. In this meaningful context, Terpsichore transcends the role of a mere symbol of artistic expression; she emerges as a guardian of the sacred feminine, inviting us to celebrate the essence of our existence. This encourages us to honor the intricate interplay of body, spirit, and earth through the vibrant and expressive art of dance, fostering a deeper connection not only to ourselves but also to the world around us. By engaging with dance, we discover pathways to liberation and self-discovery, enriching our lives and nurturing our souls in the process.

Terpsichore calls us to embrace the fluidity and grace of movement as a profound reflection of the sacred feminine that resides within each of us. She inspires us to joyfully celebrate our bodies, to find immense joy in every gesture, and to recognize that dance serves as a powerful medium of communion with the divine. It provides a unique way to express our deepest truths and connect with the very essence of life itself. Engaging in the art of dance allows women to channel these archetypes, tapping deeply into the strength, sensuality, and creativity that each goddess represents. By embodying these figures through movement, women have the opportunity to explore their own identities fully and reclaim aspects of their feminine power that may have been suppressed, overlooked, or forgotten in the complexities of modern life.

In addition to connecting with goddess archetypes, movement and dance serve as profoundly transformative rituals that honor and celebrate the sacred feminine. These practices can range from simple to elaborate, encompassing everything from intimate solo dance sessions in the comfort of the living room to vibrant group gatherings that celebrate the mystical cycles of the moon. Engaging in ritualistic movement invites women to cultivate a deep sense of mindfulness, creating a sacred space where they can authentically express their emotions, release long-held burdens, and fully embrace joy in all its forms. This intentional practice not only fosters individual healing and personal growth but also significantly contributes to collective empowerment. As women come together to share their unique experiences, they provide invaluable support for one another in their individual journeys, reinforcing the bonds of sisterhood and creating a nurturing community that uplifts everyone involved.

The healing potential of dance and movement extends far beyond the mere physical realm; it is intricately woven into the fabric of women's health, fertility, and body image. In a society that frequently imposes unrealistic and often damaging standards on women's bodies, movement emerges as a powerful avenue for reclaiming ownership of our physical selves and embracing our individuality. By immersing themselves in dances that are deeply rooted in cultural traditions or personal expression, women can cultivate a profound sense of body positivity and appreciation for their unique forms. This vital connection between the sacred feminine and the body encourages women to honor their natural cycles, celebrate their inherent uniqueness, and foster a deeper, more meaningful connection with their physical existence. In doing so, they not only empower themselves but also inspire others to embrace their own journeys of self-acceptance and healing.

The sacred feminine finds expression through movement and dance in our modern lives, serving as a powerful reminder of the divine within each of us. As adult women navigating various stages of life, we can embrace these practices to reconnect with our inner goddess, celebrate our journeys, and uplift one another. In a world that often seeks to diminish the feminine spirit, movement and dance become acts of defiance and reclamation, allowing us to rise together in celebration of the sacred feminine.

Embracing the Future

The Rise of the Sacred Feminine in Society

The resurgence of the sacred feminine in contemporary society signifies a profound and transformative shift in how we perceive and embrace the feminine principle. In a world where patriarchal narratives have long dominated and shaped our understanding of gender roles, women are actively reclaiming their voices and rediscovering the divine feminine that resides within themselves and their communities. This powerful movement is not merely a reaction against past injustices but also a vibrant celebration of the rich tapestry of feminine energy that has always existed, patiently waiting to be acknowledged and honored by society. As adult women from diverse walks of life engage with this resurgence, they discover newfound strength in the goddess archetypes that resonate deeply with their unique journeys. They draw inspiration from the timeless wisdom of ancient cultures, recognizing that these archetypes offer guidance and empowerment, illuminating the path toward self-acceptance and collective healing. This journey not only fosters individual growth but also nurtures a supportive community where women uplift one another, creating a powerful network of shared experiences and knowledge.

In exploring goddess archetypes, we uncover a rich tapestry of attributes that embody the sacred feminine. From the nurturing qualities of Gaia, who represents the earth and motherhood, to the fierce independence of Kali, a symbol of transformation and strength, these divine figures offer powerful frameworks for self-exploration and personal empowerment. Each goddess illuminates different aspects of womanhood, inviting us to reflect on our own unique experiences and journeys through life. By connecting with these archetypes, women across generations can fully embrace their multifaceted identities, acknowledging both their light and their shadow. This exploration not only encourages a deeper understanding of the divine feminine as a dynamic and vital force but also reveals it as a living, breathing energy that profoundly influences our lives and choices in countless ways. Through this connection, we can find inspiration and guidance in navigating our own paths.

Feminine spirituality practices play a crucial and transformative role in this rise, offering a variety of rituals and meditative experiences that deeply honor the sacred feminine. These practices serve not only as powerful tools for personal growth and self-discovery but also as communal gatherings that foster connection, solidarity, and empowerment among women. From moon ceremonies that celebrate the cycles of life to the mindful creation of beautiful altars, these rituals provide a sacred space for women to express their intentions, celebrate their bodies, and seek healing and rejuvenation. Engaging in these practices allows women to reclaim their bodies as sacred vessels, reinforcing the profound idea that every woman is inherently worthy of love, respect, and empowerment, thus cultivating a supportive network that uplifts all.

In recent years, there has been a noticeable and significant resurgence of interest in goddess worship and witchcraft, which is often intricately linked to themes of female empowerment, personal autonomy, and the celebration of the sacred feminine. This revival reflects a broader societal shift toward reclaiming, redefining, and embracing feminine power in a world where traditional gender roles are increasingly challenged and questioned. As more individuals explore these spiritual practices, they find a sense of community and connection that fosters a deeper understanding of the divine feminine energy.

The rise of goddess worship can be viewed as a powerful response to the entrenched patriarchal narratives that have long marginalized women's voices and contributions throughout history. In contemporary society, many individuals are increasingly turning to ancient practices and mythologies that celebrate and honor feminine divinity. They are seeking inspiration from a diverse array of goddesses across various cultures who embody qualities such as strength, wisdom, creativity, and nurturing. Figures like Kali, Isis, and Aphrodite are being revisited not merely as deities, but as potent symbols of empowerment that encourage women to embrace and explore their multifaceted identities and inherent strengths. This resurgence reflects a broader cultural shift toward recognizing the importance of feminine energy in both personal and collective spaces, fostering an environment where women's experiences and contributions are valued and celebrated.

Witchcraft, too, has emerged as a powerful and transformative avenue for self-exploration and personal expression, capturing the imaginations of many. Often associated with healing, intuition, and a profound connection to nature, modern witchcraft offers a meaningful and enriching framework for women to reclaim their agency and assert their identities with confidence. This practice frequently emphasizes the vital importance of community, ritual, and personal sovereignty, allowing individuals the freedom to delve into their spirituality on their own terms and in their own unique ways, cultivating a deeply personalized practice. The modern witch is often viewed as a figure of resistance, courageously challenging societal norms and conventions that seek to limit individual expression. In doing so, she embraces a holistic approach to femininity that deeply values emotional and spiritual well-being, fostering empowerment, self-discovery, and a sense of belonging within a diverse and supportive community.

The intersection of goddess worship and witchcraft serves as a profound and potent reminder of the sacred feminine, a rich and transformative concept that celebrates the divine qualities traditionally associated with femininity—qualities such as intuition, creativity, nurturing, and compassion. This transformative movement has beautifully fostered a deep sense of solidarity among women, creating inclusive and welcoming spaces where they can come together to share their experiences, wisdom, and mutual support. It actively encourages a meaningful and enriching reconnection with the Earth and the natural cycles of nature, promoting a more sustainable, respectful, and harmonious way of living that honors both the planet and the enduring feminine spirit. Through this collective journey, women are empowered to reclaim their rightful place within the tapestry of life, nurturing not only themselves but also the world around them.

This recent surge in popularity has been significantly amplified by the rapid rise and widespread influence of social media platforms, where vibrant and diverse communities can effortlessly form around shared interests, beliefs, and practices. These dynamic online spaces have created unique and invaluable opportunities for the widespread dissemination of knowledge, rituals, and various resources, making the concepts of goddess worship and witchcraft not only more accessible but also more engaging than ever before. In this ever-evolving digital age, a diverse array of voices from different backgrounds and experiences can actively contribute to the ongoing conversation, enriching and expanding the discourse around the sacred feminine in profound, meaningful, and transformative ways, fostering a deeper understanding and appreciation for these ancient practices.

As this vibrant movement continues to gain momentum and expand in reach, it presents a compelling challenge for individuals to thoughtfully reconsider their relationship with femininity, spirituality, and the concept of power itself. The burgeoning interest in goddess worship and witchcraft reflects not only a deeply personal journey for many individuals but also signifies a profound collective effort to redefine and reshape what it truly means to be a woman in the complexities of today's world. This powerful reclamation of the sacred feminine invites everyone to embark on a journey of self-exploration and to honor the divine qualities that reside within themselves. In doing so, it fosters a rich sense of empowerment and a deeper connection to the larger tapestry of life, encouraging a community that celebrates the multifaceted nature of femininity and spiritual expression.

The sacred feminine offers a lens through which to view healing—both personal and collective. In a time when many women grapple with issues like body image, reproductive health, and societal expectations, the teachings of the sacred feminine advocate for holistic healing approaches. Techniques such as mindfulness, energy work, and herbal medicine reconnect women with their innate wisdom and the natural cycles of life. By embracing these healing methods, women not only nurture themselves but also contribute to a broader movement of collective healing, fostering a sense of community and support that transcends individual struggles.

The rise of the sacred feminine in modern contexts illustrates how contemporary women embody and express these principles in their daily lives. Women are increasingly embracing their roles as leaders, healers, and creators, drawing strength from their connection to the divine feminine. This expression is evident in various forms—art, activism, education, and even in the way they nurture relationships. By celebrating the sacred feminine, women are not only redefining their identities but also paving the way for future generations to honor and embody this powerful energy. As we journey together in this exploration, we open the door to a world where the sacred feminine is acknowledged, celebrated, and integrated into the very fabric of our lives.

Individual and Collective Action for Empowerment

In the journey of empowerment, both individual and collective actions serve as vital catalysts for transformation within ourselves and our communities. The sacred feminine, as represented through various goddess archetypes, reminds us that empowerment is not solely a personal endeavor; it flourishes when women unite to support one another. Each goddess embodies distinct attributes—wisdom, strength, creativity, and nurturing—that inspire us to recognize our own potential. By exploring these archetypes, we can draw parallels to our lives, prompting personal reflection and encouraging us to harness our unique gifts while fostering a sense of solidarity among women.

Individual empowerment begins with self-awareness and acknowledgment of our inner goddess. Engaging in feminine spirituality practices such as meditation, journaling, or ritual can help us connect with our true selves and the divine energy that resides within. These practices allow us to cultivate a deeper understanding of our strengths and vulnerabilities, creating a foundation for growth. When we honor our own journeys, we naturally inspire those around us, leading to a ripple effect of empowerment. Each story shared, every experience embraced, becomes a thread in the larger tapestry of women's shared wisdom, illuminating the path for others.

Collective action amplifies the individual journey, creating a powerful force for change. Women gathering in circles—whether for a shared ritual, a workshop, or simply a conversation—can serve as a sanctuary where healing and empowerment take root. These gatherings not only validate our experiences but also enhance our ability to collaborate on issues affecting our lives and the world around us. As we unite in our intentions, we can address societal challenges, advocate for our rights, and uplift one another through shared experiences. In these moments of connection, we become living embodiments of the sacred feminine, nurturing and empowering one another.

The healing aspect of the sacred feminine extends beyond personal growth; it encompasses the collective healing of our communities. Women have historically been caretakers, and this role can be expanded to include active participation in social justice movements, environmental causes, and wellness initiatives. By embracing our roles as healers, we can foster environments where all women feel valued and empowered. This commitment to collective well-being honors the legacy of the goddesses who came before us, reminding us that our power is magnified when we work together for the greater good.

In modern contexts, the sacred feminine is expressed through the myriad ways women embody their divinity in daily life. From advocating for body positivity and health to exploring creative pursuits, women today are redefining what it means to be empowered. By sharing our stories and supporting one another, we celebrate the diverse expressions of the feminine divine. In doing so, we not only honor our individual journeys but also cultivate a collective spirit of resilience and empowerment that reverberates through generations. As we rise together, we embody the essence of the sacred feminine, paving the way for a brighter, more inclusive future for all women.

Creating a New Narrative: The Role of Women

In our journey towards reclaiming the sacred feminine, it is imperative to acknowledge the profound role women play in crafting new narratives that honor their experiences, values, and wisdom. Throughout history, women have often been relegated to the margins of storytelling, their voices overshadowed by patriarchal perspectives. Yet, the resurgence of interest in goddess archetypes and feminine spirituality is empowering women today to take center stage in their own stories. This subchapter invites us to explore how women can weave their unique narratives, drawing from the rich tapestry of cultural myths, spiritual practices, and personal experiences that resonate with the sacred feminine.

At the heart of this new narrative is the recognition that every woman embodies aspects of various goddess figures, from the nurturing qualities of Demeter to the fierce independence of Kali. By exploring these archetypes, women can access a deeper understanding of their own identities and strengths. Each goddess represents not just a mythological figure, but a reflection of the complexities and multifaceted nature of womanhood itself. In embracing these archetypes, women are empowered to reclaim their stories, transforming personal struggles and triumphs into a collective narrative that honors the sacred feminine in all its diversity.

Feminine spirituality practices play a crucial role in this narrative shift, offering rituals and meditations that connect women with their inner selves and the greater universe. These practices serve as a reminder of the sacredness of the feminine experience, encouraging women to honor their bodies, emotions, and intuition. Whether through moon ceremonies, creative expressions, or communal gatherings, these spiritual acts foster a sense of belonging and solidarity among women. They create spaces where stories can be shared and celebrated, allowing women to heal and empower one another through their shared experiences.

The exploration of myths and legends surrounding the sacred feminine reveals how these narratives can guide contemporary women in their personal journeys. Myths are not merely relics of the past; they are living stories that hold wisdom and insights relevant to today's challenges. By engaging with these stories, women can find inspiration and guidance in their daily lives, adapting the lessons of the past to address current realities. This process of reinterpretation not only honors the legacy of the sacred feminine but also fosters a sense of agency as women carve out their own paths in a world that often seeks to define them.

Creating a new narrative is about recognizing the

sacred feminine in every aspect of life, from health and body image to relationships and career choices. It calls for a holistic understanding of womanhood that embraces the physical, emotional, and spiritual dimensions of being a woman. As women come together to share their stories and celebrate their journeys, they contribute to a collective narrative that honors the diversity of experiences within the sacred feminine. By doing so, they not only empower themselves but also inspire future generations to embrace their own sacred narratives, ensuring that the voices of women resonate for years to come.

Visioning a Sacred Feminine Future

In envisioning a sacred feminine future, we embark on a journey that honors the myriad expressions of the divine feminine found throughout cultures and histories. This visioning process is not merely about the past; it is a powerful call to action for women of all ages and backgrounds to reclaim their sacred heritage and integrate it into their daily lives. By delving into the rich tapestry of goddess archetypes, we can find inspiration in figures like Kali, who embodies transformation, or Demeter, who represents nurturing and abundance. Each goddess serves as a guide, inviting us to tap into our unique strengths and gifts. Together, we can weave a narrative that celebrates the diverse qualities of the feminine divine, empowering us to shape our own destinies.

Feminine spirituality practices play a crucial role in this vision. Engaging in rituals, meditations, and ceremonies that honor the sacred feminine fosters a deep connection with our inner selves and with each other. These practices create sacred spaces where we can explore our emotions, release old patterns, and embrace new possibilities. Whether through a moonlit gathering to celebrate the cycles of nature or a quiet meditation that connects us to the divine within, these moments of reflection and reverence allow us to nurture our spirits. As we come together in community, we amplify our intentions, creating a collective energy that can manifest profound change in our lives and the world around us.

Healing and empowerment are essential facets of our vision for a sacred feminine future. The sacred feminine teaches us that healing is a holistic journey, encompassing not only physical well-being but also emotional and spiritual health. By embracing practices such as energy work, herbalism, and intuitive healing, we can reclaim our bodies as sacred vessels deserving of love and care. As we share our stories of struggle and triumph, we empower one another to rise above societal limitations and redefine our narratives. This collective healing fosters resilience, enabling us to confront challenges with grace and courage while uplifting those around us.

Mythology serves as a powerful lens through which we can understand and embody the sacred feminine. The stories of goddesses and heroines throughout history reveal timeless truths about the female experience—our struggles, triumphs, and the wisdom gained from navigating the world. These myths encourage us to embrace our multifaceted identities and to recognize the strength inherent in vulnerability. By studying these narratives, we find solace and inspiration in knowing that we are part of a larger tapestry of women who have walked this path before us. As we reclaim these stories, we not only honor our ancestors but also empower future generations of women to embrace their own divine journeys.

In modern contexts, the sacred feminine is expressed in diverse and transformative ways. Contemporary women are stepping into their power, embodying the principles of the divine feminine through activism, creativity, and authentic self-expression. As we navigate the complexities of the modern world, we are called to honor our bodies, our health, and our unique contributions. By celebrating our individuality while recognizing our interconnectedness, we can cultivate an inclusive community that embraces the sacred feminine in all its forms. This vision of a sacred feminine future is not limited to a singular path; rather, it is a vibrant mosaic that reflects the diverse experiences of women across time and space, inviting us all to rise together in celebration of the divine feminine within and around us.

Women's personal empowerment through the expression of femininity is a dynamic and multifaceted journey that reflects ongoing societal changes and challenges. By fully embracing femininity in all its various forms, women are not only reclaiming their identities but also paving the way for future generations to express themselves freely and authentically, without fear of judgment or restriction. As we continue to move forward in this evolving landscape, the celebration of diverse expressions of femininity will remain a vital and essential aspect of the broader movement toward gender equality and empowerment, influencing not just individual lives but also societal norms and expectations.

Woman's personal empowerment through the expression of femininity represents an evolving narrative that vividly reflects broader societal changes. As we continue to progress into the future, the concept of femininity is undergoing a profound redefinition, allowing women to embrace their identities in increasingly diverse, authentic, and meaningful ways. This significant transformation not only highlights individual journeys and personal stories but also underscores the collective movement toward greater acceptance and a deeper understanding of the varied expressions of womanhood. This evolution fosters an environment where women feel empowered to celebrate their uniqueness and contribute to a richer, more inclusive dialogue about femininity in today's world.

The concept of being labeled a "bad feminist" frequently emerges from the perceived contradictions that exist between an individual's personal preferences and the overarching ideals of feminism as a movement. A notable example of this phenomenon is the enjoyment of the color pink, which has long been linked to traditional notions of femininity and established gender roles. This historical association can create the impression that embracing the color pink somehow weakens or undermines core feminist principles. It suggests that by liking pink, one is merely conforming to societal expectations rather than actively challenging and redefining them. Such a viewpoint raises questions about the complexities of identity and the diverse ways individuals can engage with feminist ideals while still embracing elements of traditional culture.

However, this perspective can be somewhat limiting in its scope. Feminism, at its core, fundamentally revolves around the freedom to choose and express oneself authentically without the constraints imposed by societal norms and expectations. Liking the color pink does not inherently negate or undermine feminist beliefs; rather, it can be viewed as a vibrant expression of individuality and personal identity. Color preferences, much like any other personal choice, are shaped by a myriad of factors, including cultural influences, upbringing, personal experiences, and even the nuances of social interactions. Embracing such preferences can actually enrich the feminist dialogue by highlighting the diversity of choices available to individuals

Embracing pink, along with other traditionally feminine 'girly girl' elements, can serve as a remarkably powerful act of subversion. It challenges the deeply entrenched stereotype that women must entirely reject symbols of femininity in order to be taken seriously in society or to effectively advocate for gender equality. By proudly expressing a fondness for pink, individuals can reclaim the color from its stereotypical associations, transforming it into a bold and vibrant statement of empowerment rather than mere conformity. This act not only celebrates femininity in all its forms but also fosters a broader and more inclusive conversation about the complexities of gender identity and the multifaceted nature of empowerment. By redefining what it means to embrace femininity, we open up new avenues for dialogue and understanding, reinforcing the idea that empowerment can take many shapes, colors, and expressions in our diverse society

Furthermore, feminism encompasses a rich and diverse range of voices, experiences, and perspectives. It is essential to recognize that not every feminist will connect with the same symbols, aesthetics, or cultural references. Embracing and celebrating the differences in personal expression, including individual color preferences, reflects the movement's fundamental value of inclusivity and acceptance. The enjoyment of pink, for instance, does not make someone a "bad feminist." On the contrary, it reinforces the notion that feminism embraces a broad spectrum of identities and personal choices. True empowerment is derived from the freedom to love what you love, without the pressure to conform strictly to conventional feminist ideals or expectations. Each person's unique expression contributes to the richness of the feminist movement as a whole.

Historically, femininity has frequently been constrained by rigid societal norms and expectations, which have relegated women to specific roles or behaviors deemed appropriate. However, as gender norms continue to evolve and shift in contemporary society, women are increasingly reclaiming femininity on their own terms, redefining what it means to be feminine. This powerful reclamation involves recognizing that femininity is not a monolith but rather a rich and diverse spectrum of expressions that can encompass strength, vulnerability, assertiveness, compassion, and myriad other qualities. By embracing this multifaceted nature of femininity, women are forging their own identities and challenging traditional perceptions.

Fourth wave feminism, emerging in the early 2010s, is characterized by its focus on intersectionality, digital activism, and a broadening of the feminist agenda to include issues such as sexual harassment, body positivity, and the rights of marginalized communities. This wave harnesses the power of social media to mobilize grassroots movements, raise awareness, and foster solidarity among diverse groups of women and allies.

The concept of the sacred feminine intersects with fourth wave feminism by emphasizing the spiritual, intuitive, and nurturing aspects traditionally associated with femininity. This idea draws from various cultural, religious, and spiritual traditions that honor the feminine principle as a source of wisdom, creativity, and healing. The sacred feminine invites a re-examination of women's roles and contributions beyond patriarchal confines, encouraging a reclaiming of feminine identities that celebrate strength, resilience, and interconnectedness.

Integrating the sacred feminine into fourth wave feminism can enhance the movement by fostering a deeper understanding of women's experiences and promoting a holistic approach to empowerment. It encourages women to connect with their inner selves and with each other, creating a sense of community and shared purpose. This synthesis can lead to a more inclusive and compassionate feminist movement that not only addresses social and political issues but also nurtures emotional and spiritual well-being.

In the face of ongoing societal change, women are increasingly empowered to express their femininity through a wide range of avenues, including fashion, art, leadership, and activism. The rise of social media has played a particularly significant role in this empowerment, providing dynamic platforms for women to showcase their individuality and connect with others who share similar experiences, values, and aspirations. These platforms not only enable women to challenge traditional stereotypes but also encourage them to celebrate their unique expressions of femininity. This celebration can take many forms, whether it means embracing traditionally feminine traits with pride or subverting those norms altogether in bold and innovative ways, redefining what femininity can mean in contemporary society.

The conversation surrounding femininity is increasingly inclusive, acknowledging the experiences of women from diverse backgrounds, cultures, and identities. This inclusivity fosters a sense of community and solidarity among women, empowering them to support one another in their personal journeys. As society continues to evolve, the intersectionality of femininity becomes more pronounced, allowing for a richer dialogue about what it means to be a woman today.

In the modern workplace, women are increasingly asserting their femininity by adopting leadership styles that prioritize collaboration, empathy, and emotional intelligence. This significant shift challenges the long-standing notion that traditional masculine traits, such as aggression and competitiveness, are the sole pathways to achieving success. As women continue to rise and break barriers in various fields, they are actively redefining leadership to encompass qualities that have often been associated with femininity. In doing so, they are not only expanding the definition of strength and competence but also illustrating that diverse leadership approaches can lead to innovative solutions and a more inclusive work environment. This evolution reflects a growing recognition that effective leadership can take many forms, and embracing these varied styles enriches the workplace for everyone involved.

Looking ahead, the future of women's empowerment through femininity encompasses not only a significant focus on mental health and self-care but also underscores the critical importance of community support and the sharing of experiences among women. As women increasingly prioritize their well-being and personal growth, they are discovering the profound strength that emerges from expressing their emotions and vulnerabilities in a society that has historically discouraged such openness and candidness. This embrace of emotional authenticity represents a deeply powerful form of empowerment, enabling women to cultivate resilience and confidence while simultaneously fostering deeper and more meaningful connections with others in their lives, including friends, family, and colleagues.

By creating inclusive spaces for dialogue and support, women can uplift one another, building a robust network of solidarity that enhances their collective strength and creates numerous opportunities for collaboration and mentorship. Such a network not only promotes individual growth but also nurtures a culture of understanding, compassion, and shared experiences that can have a transformative ripple effect throughout society. As women engage in these supportive environments, they reinforce the notion that vulnerability is not a weakness but rather a vital source of strength that can drive meaningful change and inspire future generations to embrace their own journeys.

Through this unwavering commitment to emotional openness and community, women are paving the way for a more empowered and connected future, one where their voices are amplified and their contributions valued, leading to a more equitable society for all. This evolution towards recognizing and celebrating the power of femininity in its many forms is not just a personal journey but a collective movement that seeks to uplift all women, encouraging them to take their rightful place in shaping a better world. As this momentum continues to grow, the impact of women supporting women will resonate far beyond individual lives, creating a legacy of empowerment that will inspire countless others for years to come.

About the Author

Emeleth Morliniel holds a Third Degree in British Celtic Traditional Witchcraft. That's a fancy way of saying she spent a lot of years in witch school and underwent a lot of initiation and elevation rites, and is now considered qualified to carry out the role of High Priestess. But within her own Circle, she's usually the one managing the group's energy work and spellcraft because she's exceedingly bad at memorizing lines.

She writes fiction under the name Heather Ember Amsden, and is the author of the Evergreen Witches cozy urban fantasy series and the Everwood Tales medieval fantasy series. She lives near Lexington, Kentucky with her two cats who enjoy interrupting the creative process. On any given weekend you're likely to find her at a renaissance faire when she's not writing, sewing, or working on her handspun yarn business. She's also a sociology professor, a master seamstress, and historical costume designer. Likes: cats, coffee, and cable knit sweaters. Dislikes: stink bugs, seafood, and wet socks.

You can find updates about her books online at:
Instagram: @evergreenwitches
Facebook: @Evergreen Witches
Books2Read.com/Emeleth-Morliniel